The
Royal Winton
Collectors Handbook
From 1925
Cottage Ware, Art Deco, Lustre Ware, Pastels, etc

Muriel M. Miller

First edition

Francis Joseph
London
1998

First Edition
Francis Joseph Publishing

Typeset by E J Folkard Print Services
199 Station Road, Crayford, Kent DA1 3QF

Printed by The Greenwich Press
Standard House, Westmoor Street, London SE7.

Photography: Trevor Leak

Important Notice

All the information contained in this book has been compiled from reliable sources and every effort has been made to eliminate errors. Neither the publishers nor the author can be held responsible for losses which may occur in the purchase, sale or other transaction of items because of the information contained herein. Readers who feel they have discovered errors are invited to write and inform us so that these may be corrected in subsequent editions.

To Diana and Ken Glibbery

With gratitude for their help
and friendship

And to Dave Barker, as always

Foreword

Following our takeover of Royal Winton in 1995, it soon became apparent that we had acquired a company with a unique heritage. Alas, most of the old pattern books and catalogues have been destroyed over recent decades. Therefore when Muriel's book, *Collecting Royal Winton Chintz*, was published in 1996, it proved to be a rich source for both collectors and the company, illustrating as it does the many and varied patterns produced by Royal Winton in its heyday.

Since forming 'Grimwades Ltd, Trading as Royal Winton' on 18th October 1995, it has proved to be an exacting – yet enthralling – task to restore the company to a healthy and competitive force in the market place.

New and exciting developments are planned for 1997, starting with the introduction of a limited edition vase in the popular Florence pattern. This is based on the original lithograph design but computer enhanced in line with modern technology. We plan to follow this success with other popular patterns in shapes both new and old. Other innovative ideas are also being discussed.

Muriel's new book is informative and colourful, and bound to be of interest to collectors all over the world. It offers a fascinating look at the novel and spirited designs of the 1930s, the like of which, sadly, we may never see again.

Ian Davis
Chairman

Contents

Introduction

Since writing *Collecting Royal Winton Chintz*, I have been inundated with enquiries about the next book. Some collectors are interested in the superb lustre ware produced by Grimwades, others are keen on the Royal Winton tea ware made in plain pastel colours, while yet another group favours the cottage and relief-moulded ware. The Art deco pottery produced is also avidly collected, as are the musical and character jugs.

All these ranges were produced in the 1930s, with Byzanta lustre ware preceding this date by a few years. It was an adventurous and prolific period for the company and, after the interruption by World War II and its aftermath, was never to reach such heights of design again.

As a collector of anything and everything made by Grimwades, I have been only too pleased to venture on the task of producing a book about these varied wares. However, it has been both exciting and frustrating.

The frustration stems from the fact that little or no documentation exists to give information on the manufacturing processes or exact dates of production. Lustre ware, for example, was first made in 1925 but dates of the various patterns cannot be narrowed down further than 1925+ or, that they were produced from the 1930s onwards.

It was hoped that the publicity engendered by the Chintz book would bring forward more general information about the company with maybe some undiscovered catalogues or pattern books turning up. Unfortunately, this has not yet occurred.

When contacting other collectors or dealers regarding a certain pattern, it can be very difficult to describe it over the telephone or by fax. I have therefore adopted the same system of naming many of the patterns as I did in the Chintz book, to make for easier recognition by collectors. These names are given in quotes. Known pattern names are without quotes, the only exception being '6742', a hand painted pattern described by that number by Grimwades.

Doubtless, many more lustre patterns will come to light after publication – it happened with the Chintz book – but, hopefully, these will be included in any further editions of this book.

I make no apology for including the original text detailing the history of Leonard Grimwade and his company which appeared in the Chintz book. Many collectors interested in the wares covered by this book may not have bought the Chintz book, and will be interested in the historical details. Collectors who do have the Chintz book, but who collect other Royal Winton as well, will be relieved not to have to delve into their copy of the Chintz book for information.

Happy collecting!

Muriel M. Miller

The Company

The firm of Grimwade Brothers was founded in 1885 at the Winton Pottery, Stoke-on-Trent, by Leonard Lumsden Grimwade and his elder brother, Sidney Richard. The factory consisted of a shed sited between two rows of cottages but business was brisk and the firm expanded.

In 1887, the Winton Hotel was built as showrooms, close by Stoke Station and convenient for visiting buyers who travelled by rail. The company's turnover doubled each year and by 1890, a flourishing export department was established with the company taking a London showroom at Ely Place, Holborn.

To cope with this development of trade, the Winton Pottery was built in 1892. This was a large building set on the main road and had the added advantage of being only a three minute walk from Stoke Station. The building had a frontage of 180 feet and a four-storey elevation. It contained some of the most up-to-date equipment to be found in the potteries at that time and, over subsequent years, the area at the rear was built up with a network of kilns, ovens and workshops. The total area covered was almost two acres.

The showrooms were sited in London at 3-5 Charterhouse Street, Holborn Circus. By 1889, the company had moved to Ely Place, Holborn.

In March 1900, the Stoke Pottery, owned by James Plant, was acquired with Plant being given a place on the Grimwades Board as a director. The Stoke factory was adjacent to the Trent and Mersey Canal and, apart from the large range of ovens and kilns, also included complete equipment for milling the raw materials, including flint and Cornish stone. The three potteries (Grimwade Bros, Winton Pottery and Stoke Pottery) were then amalgamated under the title of Grimwades Limited with Leonard Grimwade as chairman.

In that same year, the Grimwade brothers left Ely Place and purchased the lease on 13 St Andrew Street, a corner site at the conjunction of St Andrew Street and Shoe Lane in Holborn Circus, London. Winton House, as it was known, became their main showroom.

Back in Stoke, Leonard Grimwade experimented with new methods of kiln-firing and developed enamel firing of high quality with the use of Climax Rotary Kilns.

New showrooms were erected at the Winton Pottery in Hanley in 1906. To achieve these, three cottages in Newland Street were pulled down and a three-storey building erected. It was opened by the Mayor of Hanley on 25th October.

Expansion continued at a great rate. Brownfield's Works, carried on by The Upper Hanley Pottery in Woodall Street, Cobridge, were acquired in 1906, the factory being 'particularly adapted for trade with Canada, the United States of America and other important foreign markets'. Later in the same year, Atlas China (formerly David Chapman & Sons) in Wolfe Street was purchased, enabling the company 'to cater for their many customers who required high-class China Tea Sets at moderate prices especially suited to a cultured taste'.

The Heron Cross Pottery at Fenton, owned by Messrs Hines Bros, was an extensive earthenware pottery manufactory with extra large ovens and several enamel kilns and this was bought the following year, adding considerably to the company's facilities. (It was later sold to Cartwright & Edwards in 1916.) Grimwades also acquired the Rubian Art Pottery Ltd in 1913.

Export trade was also on the up with the company having agents in Australia, New Zealand, Canada, India, South Africa, South America, United States of America, Sweden, Norway and Germany. By 1920, Egypt had been added to the list.

In 1908, Leonard Grimwade bought shares in the Chromo Transfer and Potters' Supply Co Ltd. This company, which was situated at one end of the Winton Pottery factory, provided 'chromo and lithographic transfers, ceramic colours, potters' materials, glazes and the like'. They were also responsible for the development of 'Duplex' paper, a thin printing tissue which make the lithographing process easier.

Leonard Grimwade also purchased the patent rights of the Grimwade Rotary Display stands around 1913. These were 'Made of finest steel, double-plated metal parts, stained wood shelves' and could accommodate '12 half tea sets, 12 cover dishes and plates, or 12 ewers and basins'. The stands were used for shop display and economised on space. Also, 'ware can be displayed so effectively that assistants are able to increase sales and serve customers far more expeditiously.'

Patent 'Ideal' Display Blocks & Wires were also acquired by Grimwades, and these were used to show tea cups and saucers to advantage, or sets of jugs,

Stoke Pottery, c1930

blancmange moulds, teapots and butter dishes. Smaller blocks were used for trios (cup, saucer and tea plate) or samples of dinner ware. Wall mounted hardwood strips were available for displaying wash stand sets.

In 1920 a laboratory was set up at the Victory Works at the Stoke Pottery. This was run under the supervision of Leonard Grimwade's son, Charles Donovan, who had for some years been in charge of a large tile and brick works at Tongshan, North China. Grimwades anticipated cheaper production, improved quality and to test new methods and new materials 'so that we may be in a strong position for future business.' Also that year, gas fired tunnel ovens were pioneered by Grimwades. These had been laid just after the Armistice and were opened in September 1920. The huge tunnels, 298 feet in length, were capable of turning out as much ware as had formerly six full-sized ovens.

The railway strike in 1920 affected delivery of goods to customers, so Leonard Grimwade purchased a new 'Karrier' motor lorry for a cost of £1300. This proved so successful – 'No breakage – no delay – no incivility on the part of carters and a lessening of serious inconveniences' – that the company aimed to build up a complete system of motor transport during 1921.

In 1929, a new showroom was set up at Winton House in Stoke-on-Trent. It was named the Victoria Showroom and was to be used for tableware of all kind, bowls, vases and jardinières. 'It will be used exclusively for representative selections of the latest and most artistic productions', ran the advertisement. It was to be the third showroom at Winton House. The Royal Showroom catered for the dinner ware, toilet ware, teapots and coffee sets and so on, while the Excelsior Showroom was devoted to clearance lines suitable for sales.

Leonard Grimwade died in 1931 with James Plant (Senior) dying in the same year. Plant's son, another James, took over as Managing director in 1933 and he died in 1962.

The Rubian Art factory ceased production during World War II and was used only for storage. At the same time, the Atlas China factory was also closed, apart from storage purposes, and the building later became unsafe.

In January 1964, the company was taken over by the Howard Pottery Co Ltd of Shelton. Part of Grimwades production (50 per cent of which was exported mainly to Australia, Canada and New Zealand) was moved from Stoke to Norfolk Street, Shelton, with the remainder being transferred some weeks later. The name Royal Winton was kept.

The ware made was highly ornamental and much of it was hand painted. There was also a great proportion of gold fancies made, with a specially air conditioned room being set aside for the application of the gold. Orders went out all over the world. Canada formed the largest overseas market, with Australia and New Zealand close behind. A new 'Royal Winton' tie-on label had been designed and this was printed in the Howard colours of chocolate brown, white and grey.

Between 1964 and the present day there have been several successive owners of Royal Winton. Pentagon Holdings acquired Howard Pottery in late 1960, and supplied Taunton Vale Industries with ware. Pentagon itself went on the market in 1973 and was bought by its erstwhile customer, Taunton Vale Industries Ltd. In 1979 the Staffordshire Potteries purchased Taunton Vale Industries and in

1986 were themselves taken over by Coloroll (Ceramics Division). Despite all the various takeovers, the name Royal Winton was kept alive.

When Coloroll was declared bankrupt in 1990/91 there was a management buy-out for Royal Winton. In 1993, the company was purchased by Spencer Hammer Associates and a new company formed, Burnan International Limited.

In 1995, Royal Winton became part of the Taylor Tunnicliffe Group and in October of that year brought back the Grimwade name by registering the company as Grimwades, trading as Royal Winton. It is to be hoped that, once again, the Royal Winton name will be one of excellence.

View of the Finishing Warehouse taken in 1906.

Leonard L. Grimwade

Leonard Lumsden Grimwade was a man of extraordinary vitality and enthusiasm, and the driving force behind Grimwades Royal Winton Pottery. *The North Staffordshire Echo* profiled him in 1907, describing him as 'quick in all his movements, restless in activity, audacious in projects, with fine imagination and generous sentiments, he is an interesting personality and an admirable ally.'

Lily Bell, who worked at Winton Potteries during the 1920s and 1930s said, 'Leonard Grimwade, he was absolutely alive. He was full of it. No sooner than he'd thought anything, he was off – he was like a bottle of pop; got to be doing.'

Leonard Grimwade was born in Ipswich in 1864, the youngest of nine children. Large families were then quite common; Leonard's father, Richard Grimwade (1816-1905), was one of 15 children, while his uncle, Edward, produced 17 children. Leonard's grandfather, William Grimwade (1782-1856), was a Suffolk man who owned Poplar Farm at Wetheringsett, some 16 miles from Ipswich. Amy Langdon, Leonard Grimwade's mother, was a woollen draper at the time of her marriage.

At 16, Leonard moved to Hanley in North Staffordshire where he worked for his uncle, Edward, as a 'dry-salter'. According to a contemporary dictionary, the term dry-salter had two definitions: a dealer in dried and salted meats, pickles and sauces, or a dealer in dye stuffs, chemical products etc. As Leonard's uncle was a chemist, it can be assumed that the boy worked with chemicals rather than pickles.

By 1880, however, he was working as a decorator and modeller in the potteries. He soon began to show signs of the restless energy and dynamism that were to characterise him in later life and, shortly before he was 21, he opened his own business as a factor, the manufacturing side being developed gradually. His first premises consisted of no more than a shed in a yard, sited between two rows of cottages but, before long, he was in a position to invite his elder brother Sidney Richard Grimwade, a potter, to join him in his venture. And so, in 1885, the firm of Grimwade Brothers was founded. Around the late 1880s, another Grimwade brother, Edward Ernest, joined the firm. He was later to represent the company's interests in Australasia, leaving England in 1905 to live in New Zealand.

In 1886, Leonard returned to Ipswich to marry Marion Cooper (1865-1925).There were three children of the marriage: a son, Charles Donovan Grimwade (1890-1971), and two daughters, Elsie (born in 1892) and Muriel (born in 1907) It appeared to have been a happy marriage. The Grimwades celebrated their silver wedding anniversary in style in 1911 when family members, colleagues and employees, in all numbering some 900 people, filled the Victoria Hall at Hanley. The *Staffordshire Sentinel* reported that the couple had been presented with a silver rose bowl and two silver vases, a gift from their employees.

There was another reason for the celebration, the *Staffordshire Sentinel* declared. 'It was primarily a recognition by the firm of the loyalty of its employees during the rush of orders attendant upon the Coronation.'

Leonard Grimwade's reply to the presentation threw light on his early days as a manufacturer. When he wooed and won his wife all those years ago, he said, the business of Grimwades Ltd was in its infancy. The whole work of the firm was carried on in one small warehouse, and he was the warehouseman, ledger clerk, and sometimes the packer. This statement was greeted with much laughter and applause.

Marion Grimwade died in 1925 and Leonard remarried shortly afterwards. His new wife, Minnie, presented him with a baby girl, Janet, in 1927.

Charles Donovan Grimwade was to follow his father into the pottery business. He left school at 17 and worked at the Shelton laboratory in 1908, later moving to the Atlas works. When he was twenty, he was presented with a bronze medal by the County Borough of Stoke-on-Trent. The inscription reads: Higher Education Committee. Examination in Pottery. Charles Donovan Grimwade. 2nd Place Honours Grade 1910-11.

Shortly after taking the examination, Charles Donovan went to China in 1912, where he was in charge of the Chinese Mining and Engineering Company. Based in Tongshan, North China, the works was spread over two acres and manufactured tiles and stonework piping as well as bricks. Charles Donovan was responsible for reporting on the state of affairs in clay mining, works machinery and output, as well as estimating the quantities needed, weight and cost, and time of manufacture for articles produced.

He left Tongshan in December 1915 to join the army. He left for Petrograd via the Trans-Siberian Railway, then travelling by sledge to the Swedish railway (in the Arctic winter) then on to Bergen in Norway. He reached England on 13th January 1916. He received a commission and went first to Egypt, then Palestine, being present at the capture of Jerusalem.

After the war, he became scientific advisor to Grimwades, and was soon on the Board of Directors. He married Nora Gibson in 1920. She was the daughter of Arthur Gibson who was well known for his manufacture of teapots. The couple had one daughter, Stella Ruth.

Charles Donovan's work in China appears to have been recognised by his father, as several shape names bear reference to the oriental. The 1918 catalogue, for example, shows a Tientsin toilet set and a Tongshan vase. The war years were also commemorated in the same catalogue, with toilet ware having shape names such as Belgium and Somme.

As the silver wedding celebration showed, Leonard Grimwade was known as a kindly employer. In 1892, *The Pottery Gazette* recorded a New Year's Day party at Grimwades. 'In one of the large rooms at the new works, which had been tastefully decorated for the occasion, a sumptuous repast had been spread...A lengthy programme of music – vocal and instrumental – readings, dancing and various games, gave pleasure to all.'

Several employees who worked at Royal Winton during the 1930s and earlier mentioned the room resembling a ballroom that was at the top of the building. 'It (the ballroom) was massive. There were great wide stairs and a lovely wooden banister,' one worker said. 'It looked to me as though it had been a place that had had a lot of money spent on it years ago. Upstairs it was very nice. We used to practise (dancing) there in our lunch time.' Another worker recalled the sprung maple floor and lamented the day it was turned into a showroom for toilet and dinner ware.

The girls entered into the spirit of Christmas at the factory. Florence Dennis remembers how they made paper decorations. 'We decorated the shop with crêpe paper we bought for tuppence a roll. We made orchids on a steel knitting needle and hung them all around, all the loveliest colours. I'll never forget it. And Leonard Grimwade came in and he said, "Fairyland! It's fairyland. Beautiful''. He walked through in his plus-fours; he was a grand old man.'

At the turn of the century, business was booming and the export trade was brisk. The year 1900 saw the acquisition of the Stoke Pottery and Grimwades Ltd was established, while a new showroom was set up in London. Between 1901 and 1907, four more potteries were bought out and added to the Grimwades Group.

In 1906, Grimwades took out a full page advertisement in *The Pottery Gazette* in order to contradict 'Two Representatives of Earthenware Manufacturers in Staffordshire who have persistently published malicious statements to the effect that we are not Manufacturers, but only Decorators or Factors. We have been compelled to take out Legal Proceedings in order to prevent such innuendoes.' The statement went on: 'We are just publishing a little "brochure'' explaining the chief processes carried on in making pottery.'

The brochure was ostensibly printed to commemorate the opening of the new showrooms at Winton Pottery on 25th October 1906, but would have had a secondary purpose of squashing any further talk or rumours. The booklet, entitled 'A Short Description of the Art of Potting ... as carried on by Grimwades Ltd at Winton, Stoke, Elgin & Upper Hanley Potteries', is well illustrated with scenes showing the clay presses in the slip house, the potters' shop, the 'biscuit' warehouse and so on. Some of the photographs were later used for a commemorative catalogue issued in 1913.

The company was awarded a gold medal award for some of its Hygienic Patented Ware in 1911, at the Festival of Empire, Imperial Exhibition and Pageant.

King George V and Queen Mary visited the Potteries in 1913 and Grimwades issued a catalogue commemorating the royal visit. This gave a short history of the firm as well as illustrating their ware. In addition, photographs (taken from the 1906 booklet) showed interiors of the dinner ware showroom, the toilet ware showroom, warehouses and the mould makers' shop. It also illustrated how employees carried out skills such as plate making, aerographing, gilding and enamelling.

During their visit, the royal couple toured numerous factories before attending an exhibition at the King's Hall in Stoke-on-Trent. *The Pottery Gazette* reported in their June edition that 'Grimwades had the largest individual exhibit in the whole display'.

The company were showing their new 'Jacobean' ware, a vine-leafed pattern which was a copy of early 17th century tapestry. Also featured was 'Royal Hampton', a pattern taken from old Queen Anne chintz, and 'executed in pink, black and green'. 'Royal Dorset' was another new pattern and this consisted of massed roses on a black ground.

The Queen was apparently delighted to purchase a Grimwades Winton teaset in the new 'Queen Mary Chintz'. She was also pleased to receive a gift of the Mecca Foot Warmer (a type of oval ceramic hot water bottle) in the Jacobean pattern. Leonard Grimwade, never one to miss a promotional opportunity, later used a full colour illustration of this in a catalogue describing the foot warmer as, 'Graciously accepted by Her Majesty the Queen'. An ornate gold and red crown decorates the head of the page.

Two days later, the exhibition was moved to Harrods' Stores in London and from there, went to the Liverpool Trades Exhibition.

The year 1920 was a year of change. Grimwades purchased a new 5-ton 'Karrier' motor lorry, costing £1,300. The company also installed gas-fired tunnel ovens which were to be 'lit-up' in September of that year. The famous 'Quick-Cooker' was now being made in aluminium instead of semi-porcelain as before. A research laboratory was erected at the Victory Works (part of the Winton Works) with Charles Donovan Grimwade supervising it.

A catalogue for this period sounds a hopeful note: 'The War has so completely revolutionised industry that we embrace the opportunity which reconstruction offered for the complete reorganisation of our six factories. The introduction of new and approved methods of 'MASS PRODUCTION', whereby orders can be despatched more promptly and output can be increased, has enabled us to give greater satisfaction to customers and employees alike.'

Grimwades now employed well over a thousand workers and a Managers' Council was set up by the company to form a link between the directors and the staff in order to increase efficiency.

Further care was taken of workers. The 1920 catalogue reports that: 'A charming bungalow at Ashley Heath has, by the kindness of Mr & Mrs L.L. Grimwade, been placed at the disposal of the "Welfare Work" and any of our workers needing a rest or country air, can have a few days there to recuperate ... Many have been completely set up and strengthened for the duties of life at this bracing spot. Already the health of our workers has so improved that frequently it is difficult to find even 3 or 4 out of 1500 employees who need the recreative benefits which this institution provides.'

The Ashley Heath bungalow was the site of a works outing in Easter of that year, when 85 employees sat down to tea and enjoyed sports and games on the heath.

Leonard Grimwade kept his finger on the pulse of his empire, and he travelled extensively, visiting the United States, Canada, Italy, Germany, Switzerland, Norway, Belgium, Holland, Egypt and Australia. Compelled by his restless energy to realise the value of time, he was one of the earliest motorists and drove his own car.

He was a Liberal free-trader and served on the Stoke-on-Trent County Borough Council. He was also a Justice of the Peace for Staffordshire and Secretary of the Potteries Association for the Promotion of Federation. When examined during the passing of the Federation Bill through Parliament he was asked where he lived. 'I sleep in Wolstanton,' came the reply, 'but I live in the Potteries.'

Perhaps his words make a fitting epitaph for such a man. He died as he had lived – at top speed – in a car crash when on his way to the factory on the 26th January 1931. Accompanied by his nephew, who was in the passenger seat, Leonard Grimwade failed to avoid a bus at crossroads. He died almost instantaneously. He was buried at Hartshill Cemetery.

A report in *The Pottery Gazette* stated: 'There was a big cortège, representing all sections of the local life of the Potteries, and the floral tributes were eloquent of the sense of loss which, by the passing of Mr Grimwade, the district has sustained.'

Products

Early Grimwades catalogues, dating from 1888, show a range of useful domestic items. The company concentrated mainly on toilet sets, comprising wash stand jugs, wash bowls, toothbrush vases, soap and sponge dishes, and chamber pots. They also made matching trinket sets, composed of trays, chamber or candlesticks, trinket pots, pin trays and ring stands.

They also manufactured table ware and the range was extensive with dinner and tea ware being produced in a variety of patterns and shapes, together with additional items such as cheese dishes, bacon dishes, biscuit boxes and sardine dishes.

More mundane products were also made, such as the Hygienic Hospital and Nurseryware. This ware consisted of bedpans (including one with an airtight lid for the use of typhoid patients), and urinals (*sic*) for both male and female use, children's chamber pots, slop pails, sick-feeders and ceramic hot water bottles. For the housewife, they produced jelly and blancmange moulds, fluted pudding bowls for turning out ribbed sponge puddings, lemon squeezers, pie funnels and square pie dishes (known as bakers) of various sizes which fitted neatly into one another.

The range of patented products was both wide and ingenious. The Paragon coffee pot had a removable strainer, while the Patent Tea Machine had a valve operated infuser. The Safety Milk Bowl had an incurving rim to prevent spillage when carried. The contents of the bowl were guaranteed safe from flies. 'Those who study the habits of flies', wrote *The Pottery Gazette*, 'say they would not enter the bowl by means of the curved rim – but that the slope of the spout forms a ready convenient passage of which they make good use.' Leonard Grimwade solved the problem by the addition of a patented spout cover which fitted over the spout, thus preventing any contamination. The design was awarded a Gold Medal in 1911.

The Patent Pie Dish was practically fireproof and a guarantee was given that the contents of the dish would not burn, due to a series of ring grooves at the bottom of the dish.

In 1909, the Patent Quick-Cooker Bowl was introduced and this had the virtue of doing away with unhygienic pudding cloths tied over a bowl by having a grooved ceramic lid which could be fastened down with string. The Quick-Cooker was available in no fewer than five sizes.

But perhaps the most ingenious and attractive of all was the patent hygienic Toilet 'Holdall'. This was a large shell shaped dish which would have stood between a set of two toilet jugs and basins. The 'Holdall' was divided into five sections and held two cakes of soap, two nail brushes, and a sponge. There were also four ringed holders for toothbrushes.

In 1902, the two Climax kilns were working overtime, turning out 15,000 commemorative mugs and beakers every 24 hours in preparation for the coronation of Edward VII. Grimwades claimed that at least five million mugs and beakers would be needed for the British Isles and, judging by their advertising, it would appear that the company were quite prepared to make every one of them.

Some of the prettiest toilet ware was made by Grimwades in the early 1900s, with the Nautilus toilet set being relief moulded in an attractive shell shape. The jug had a handle at the top instead of at the side, as was customary. 'Oh, how easily it pours!' proclaimed the advertisement.

Many chintz patterns were being produced, and Jacobean, Hampton, and Spode Chintz were all greatly admired by Her Majesty Queen Mary when, with King George V, she visited the Potteries in 1913. Matching trinket sets were available with the toilet sets, but what took the Queen's fancy was the new 'Mecca' Foot Warmer or hot water bottle and, according to contemporary accounts, she was delighted to be presented with one in the Jacobean pattern. The foot warmer had a patent screw top, designed by Charles Donovan Grimwade, and a tasselled silk cord was tied into holes on either side of the neck for ease of carrying.

The Pottery Gazette eulogised over the toilet ware produced by Grimwades and much comment was made about the skilful modelling, the fine selection of shapes and delicate colours used.

It is sometimes thought that it was at around this period that Royal Winton adopted the prefix Royal to the Winton trade name. A press release issued some years ago by a development and promotion group wrongly asserts that the prefix was added in 1930 when the Royal couple visited the potteries. This is obviously incorrect, as the visit was in 1913, but such inaccuracies are often passed on and are taken as gospel.

In actual fact, the Home Office, whose records go back to 1897, can find no trace of Grimwades applying for or receiving permission to use the word 'royal' as a prefix. And, far from the use of the title dating from 1913, a catalogue for 1897 (when the firm was still trading as Grimwade Brothers) shows a full colour illustration for 'Royal Winton Ware'. This shows tea and coffee pots, cocoa jugs, beer or milk sets, cruets, egg sets, cups and saucers and pillar candlesticks made in plain colours of celadon, terracotta, ivory and beige, banded with contrasting colours of sage green, brown and turquoise blue.

However, the name Royal Winton does not appear on ware until about 1917/18 when Royal Winton Ware was produced. It then vanished again, not being used until about 1929, when Grimwades took out a full page advertisement in *The Pottery Gazette* introducing their new Octron vegetable dish made in Royal Winton Ivory.

Leonard Grimwade ensured maximum publicity for his company. He advertised widely in the trade papers, invited journalists to inspect the new showrooms as they were opened, and exhibited at trade fairs. His strategy worked and *The North Staffordshire Echo* commented that Mr Grimwade had 'succeeded in establishing one of the largest businesses in the Potteries' with 'agencies or branches all over the world and is a marvel of organisation and energy.'

The first 'novelty' ware appeared around 1907 with the introduction of nursery ware decorated with illustrated quotations from nursery rhymes, while 'Brownies' ('quaint and amusing figures') adorned heraldic china. World War I saw the introduction of 'Patriotic' Ware, with each article stamped 'Made by the girls of Staffordshire during the Great War, when the Boys were in the trenches fighting for Liberty and Civilization'. The 'Bairnsfather' Souvenir Ware was also made at this time and carried 'photographic reproductions of Captain Bairnsfather's inimitable Cartoons of the Great War'.

In 1922, another range of nursery ware, this time featuring 'Black Cats' appeared, together with 'Imps' and an updated version of 'Brownies'. These were followed in 1925 by 'Aesop's Fables', 'Robinson Crusoe', 'Old Country Nursery Rhymes', 'Bubbles' and 'Piggies'.

Art and novelty wares were not neglected, either, and these ranged from tobacco jars, in scenic designs or old chintz patterns, to jardinières, similarly decorated.

In 1925, a range of lustre ware was introduced under the name of Byzanta. This was made in rich colours of tangerine, powder blue, marone (wine red or maroon), cyclamen, yellow and turquoise. The new ware proved popular and the range was expanded to take in vases of every shape and size, fruit bowls, jardinières, toilet ware and some table ware. It was reintroduced in 1937.

Grimwades introduced their new chintz ware in 1928, and this was manufactured on a large scale from the late 1920s, and well into the 1950s. It featured small, tightly grouped floral patterns that were applied to the pottery in sheet or all-over fashion. Over 80 recorded patterns and many unnamed patterns have been discovered and have proved to be highly collectable. (See: *Collecting Royal Winton Chintz* by Muriel M. Miller)

The company pioneered several new ranges of relief-modelled ware in 1933 with cottage ware appearing in 1934.

During World War II, an effort was made by all the potteries to increase export sales and this drive was spearheaded by Gordon Forsyth, the former principal of the Burslem School of Art, and a designer of considerable ability. He recruited successful designers such as Mabel Leigh, Eric Tunstall, Norma Smallwood and Billy Grindy and the Winton Potteries set up two studios for their use. Mabel Leigh, who had done such excellent work for Shorters, worked there between 1939 and 1945, and produced many strikingly lovely lustred patterns in strong, yet subtle colours. Much of her work was never fully exploited, the right market seemingly never being found.

Gordon Forsyth, known affectionately as 'Fuzzy', also worked with lustres at Grimwades, using silver and copper lustres to achieve dramatic abstract patterns and designs reminiscent of those produced for Pilkington's Royal Lancastrian ware with rampant dragons and leaping deer. He also experimented with scraffito patterns.

Norma Smallwood was best known for her tapestry designs, while Billy Grindy modelled the Royal Winton character jugs, based on wartime personalities.

In April 1940 *The Pottery Gazette* praised the new range of Rosebud ware made in plain underglaze colours of pink, green, cream and yellow. Other flowers were added to the range, such as petunias, honey lilies, pansies, briar (roses), fuchsias and tea roses.

After the War, Polish refugees were employed by Grimwades at the Elgin factory.

The hand painted ware they produced was in the style of paintings by the famous still-life painter, William Hunt, and pieces can be found with anemones superbly depicted.

In the 1950s, in an effort to combat the recession that had succeeded the post-war boom, and which had destroyed the chintz market, Royal Winton produced a range of items in gold and silver lustre. They also reintroduced their coloured lustre ware, but this was a pale imitation of the rich lustres that had been made in former years. The takeover by Howard Potteries in 1964 proved to be the death-knell of exciting, innovative designs.

Cottage Ware

This ware featured various cottages, inns and water mills and appears to have been introduced in 1929, when the Anne Hathaway series was mentioned in *The Pottery Gazette* in September of that year. Cottage ware was mentioned again in January 1934, when *The Pottery Gazette* wrote, 'The "Old English Cottage" series, of which considerable quantities have been despatched in recent months, is about to be represented in a new guise, namely as a line of old ivory. To those people, who have a leaning towards something novel, but who are not enamoured of ultra-gay colourings, this new treatment will unquestionably appeal.'

In September 1934 *The Pottery Gazette* published a photographic illustration of Ye Olde Inne, showing a plate, jam pot, sugar shaker and 3-piece condiment set.

The trade fair at Olympia in 1935 was reported in the trade papers. It was evidently well-attended and Queen Mary purchased several pieces of cottage ware from the Ann Hathaway's Cottage and Ye Olde Mill series, the latter having recently been introduced.

Always great innovators and believers in advertising, Grimwades offered some of their ware as premiums i.e. customers would collect wrappers from various food items, chocolate, for example, and be able to send off to Grimwades to redeem these against a cheaper purchase of various wares. A four-piece teaset in Ye Olde Inne, and comprising teapot, hot water jug, cream and sugar, has been found bearing a Nestlé's label tied on with silk ribbon.

The cottage ware was hand painted and this can give subtle variations to the designs, as one paintress's work was never exactly like another's. The pottery was intended for use at the table and generally comprised four-piece teasets (teapot, hot water jug, cream jug and sugar bowl), milk jugs, biscuit barrels, cheese and butter dishes, jam and preserve pots, cruets (salt and pepper) and condiments sets (salt, pepper and mustard), sugar shakers and dessert plates (now more popularly used as decorative wall plates). More rarely found are tea cups, saucers and plates, and table lamp bases.

There are five designs in cottage ware: Anne Hathaway's Cottage, Olde England, Shakespeare's Birthplace, Ye Olde Inne and Ye Olde Mill. Olde England is generally found bearing the Grimwades Rubian Art backstamp.

Ann Hathaway's Cottage (picture page 49)

Date of manufacture 1929+
Pattern Number 6605 (Tea plate), 6805 (cruet)
Registered number: Registration applied for
Backstamp 24 sometimes accompanied by BRITISH and REGN APPLIED FOR.

This series first made its appearance in 1929 and was commented on by *The Pottery Gazette* in their September issue. 'Those dealers,' they wrote, 'who have a call for useful and ornamental ware for the souvenir trade should make a point of seeing the new "Anne Hathaway" ware of Grimwades Ltd., which comprises a series of pretty views in on-glaze colourings, depicting scenes from Shakespeare's country, applied upon a maize-tinted background.'

It was also mentioned in *The Pottery Gazette* in 1935 when Queen Mary bought a quantity at the trade fair in Olympia. An invoice dated 21st February 1939 shows that the Queen purchased two teapots at a cost of two shillings (10p) each and two cheeses for one shilling and ninepence (about 8½p) each.

Anne Hathaway was a Stratford girl who married William Shakespeare in 1582. She was some eight years older than her husband and bore him three children; Susanna in 1583 and twins, Hamnet and Judith, in 1585. According to the *Encyclopedia Britannica*, Anne was the daughter of Richard Hathaway and 'was mentioned in the will of a Richard Hathaway of Shottery (a hamlet near Stratford) who died in 1581, being then in possession of the farmhouse known as "Anne Hathaway's Cottage".'

For some reason, Grimwades missed the final 'e' from her name and the backstamp bears the incorrect spelling.

Plates show a long, half-timbered house with a thatched roof. This is usually of a straw colour but examples can be found with the thatch in a blue-grey colour streaked with red. To the front of the house is seen a typical cottage garden with a profusion of bushes and plants painted in blues and pinks. A wooden gate is set into a hedge and is open to the road.

Teapots and biscuit barrels are upright in shape and appear to feature just part of the cottage. The thatched roof is stepped and the chimney is also stepped. The mullioned windows are picked out in blue and a tree coloured in pink, yellow and green is set by the front door. Cottage-garden flowers border the base of the piece. The teapot handle is green and formed from the branches of another tree.

Smaller items such as covered butter or cheese dishes, cruets, condiment sets and sugar shakers are sometimes less well decorated, the colours being harsher and the modelling rather more crude.

Olde England   (picture page 50, 51)

Date of manufacture c1930s
Backstamp 23

This series was produced by Rubian Art, a subsidiary company of Grimwades Ltd. The cottage featured bears certain similarities to Anne Hathaway's Cottage, both being half-timbered buildings with straw-coloured thatched roofs and mullioned windows picked out in blue. The Rubian Art modelling is less fine, however, and the painting rather less well done.

The wall plates are perhaps the most attractive items, being well-detailed and featuring a cottage fronted by a garden and flanked with a brick wall and a fence. A woman stands on the right of the scene and, a little further to the right, a farm vehicle of some sort which could be mistaken for a tractor, but is more likely to be a horse-drawn hay wagon. The dessert plates can differ in colour and have been found in both a yellow and pink colourway.

A contemporary catalogue describes the ware as 'A distinct novelty for table use. The modelling is in high relief and the colour work done by hand'.

Shakespeare's Birthplace   (picture page 51)

Date of manufacture c 1930s
Backstamp 25

This design may have formed part of the Anne Hathaway series, but there is no information to corroborate this. The scene has been found depicted only on plates so far, and features a long, half-timbered Elizabethan house with mullioned windows. The house is bounded by a low picket fence and fronts a highway complete with pavement and road.

The colours are subdued; the roof is streaked dully in blue and magenta, the windows are a pale blue, while the walls and fence are picked out in beige and brown. The only real touch of colour comes from the greenery in the garden.

Ye Olde Inne   (picture page 52)

Date of manufacture 1934
Registered number 819286
Backstamp 26 sometimes with the addition of the word GRIMWADES or BRITISH.

Sometimes known to collectors as The Swan Inn, the building featured is a half-timbered public house or inn. The painting is dramatic with the timbering picked out in black against creamy yellow walls. There appear to be two colourways for the roof; scarlet with some greenery or a greyish lavender highlighted in scarlet. The name of the inn is Ye Olde Swan and this can be found above the front door, along with the picture of a white swan.

In the 4-piece teaset, the building is shown as diamond-shaped, with the front door set on the corner. In biscuit barrels, however, the building is square, with the front door set between two blue mullioned windows. Protruding supports for the wicker handle are portrayed as lanterns.

Dessert plates feature the inn sign as swinging away from the door; also shown are four geese and a war memorial standing on part of a village green.

The 4-piece teaset was offered as a premium and the silk ribbons which secure the lids of the teapot and hot water jug to the bases carry a gilded label for Nestlé.

In 1937, H.M. Queen Mary ordered several items in the new colouring of Ye Olde Inne, namely, dessert plates, cheese dishes, teapots and 3-piece cruets.

Ye Olde Mille

(picture page 53)

Date of manufacture 1935

Registered number 803446

Backstamp 27 sometimes with the addition of GRIMWADES or BRITISH. Also found with the words REGISTRATION APPLIED FOR

The first mention of this design appears in *The Pottery Gazette* in April 1935 when it was reported that several pieces of Ye Olde Mill were purchased by Queen Mary at the trade fair at Olympia.

The mill featured is a water mill, the water wheel being a prominent part of the design. In the teapot (which has an underplate similar to that of the covered butter dish), the wheel is set to the front of the piece, the handle is formed by the hoist set above large wooden double doors. The reverse shows a small door set between two blue painted windows, with another window above. Trees surround the building and form an integral part of the design.

The covered butter dish also has a painted hoist and the wheel is set to the side. The base is painted to indicate a stream and cobbled paths leading to the doors. The dessert plate shows the water mill set in a meadow, backed by trees and fronted by a rushing stream. Smaller pieces, such as cream jugs leave out the mill wheel, while, with cruets, only one piece features the wheel.

There are two versions of Ye Olde Mill: one having a red roof, the other a pink roof. However, the red-roofed version is not so well-modelled and the painting is not so attractive.

Relief-Moulded Ware

The relief-moulded ware, produced by Grimwades under the Royal Winton and Rubian Art trade names, is arguably the most innovative and fanciful of all ware that was produced from the mid-1930s onwards, and featured such diverse modelling as pixies, beehives and cockerels.

The ware, known to the trade as 'Fancies' consisted principally of items for the afternoon tea table, such as teapots, cream and sugar sets, butter and cheese dishes, toast racks, cake plates and comports, sugar shakers and so on. Large jugs, vases, fruit bowls and baskets were also made in some of the ranges.

The moulding was generally crisp and well-modelled, the colours appealing. Some ranges were introduced in the plain cream colour of the new Royal Winton Ivory, only later being hand painted.

The first relief moulded ware made its appearance fairly modestly in the autumn of 1929 with the introduction of the Anne (incorrectly spelled as Ann by Grimwades) Hathaway ware (see chapter on Cottage Ware). This was closely followed in the spring of 1930 by a range of salad, cucumber and cress ware which was initially decorated with green leafage and red tomatoes.

Primula was introduced by the Rubian Art Pottery in 1933, followed by Regina, which was manufactured by both the Royal Winton and Rubian Art factories and can carry either backstamp. Gera was issued by Royal Winton and appeared in 1934.

The success of the Ann(e) Hathaway ware saw a whole series of relief moulded being introduced, with Lakeland being made in 1935. Pixie, Chanticleer and 'Dovecot' made their appearance the following year, while Terrace and Beehive were made in 1937, with Trellis Rose Garden and Peony following on in 1938.

In 1939, the range of salad ware was expanded to include relief modelled vegetables in naturalistic colours.

There were other series of relief moulded ware produced which, unfortunately cannot be dated with any accuracy, other than they were made during the years between 1929 and 1939 and bear the Royal Winton backstamp for this period. Some of the designs have been found only as jam or preserve pots, although other items may well have been made. Some series, although illustrated in the trade papers of the time as consisting of a great many items, do not appear to have actually been made in any quantity and are rarely found today. This apparent lack of production could have been due to the impending war in 1939; alternatively, it is possible the series were produced for export only.

Most of the designs were named by Grimwades and were marked on the base of these. Some, however, remain unknown. For ease of identification, these designs have now been given working titles which are printed in quotes.

'Apple' (picture page 54)

Date of manufacture 1934+ .
Backstamp 7

So far, this has been found only in the form of a lidded preserve pot on a fast (integral) stand. It was described as 'Jam pot No. 16 (Honey)' in an invoice dated 1939, when H.M. Queen Mary ordered 12 of these – which suggests that the pot would be used for honey rather than a preserve.

The base consists of rosy apples, realistically painted and interspersed with leaves in a rich green. The lid depicts apple tree leaves with a stalk forming the knob or finial.

Beehive (picture page 54, 55)

Date of manufacture 1936
Pattern numbers 3284, 4070 (primrose colourway); 6822 (tan colourway)
Backstamp 7, 28

This relief moulded design is perhaps one of the most popular with collectors. The series was first mentioned in the trade press in October 1937: 'A unit which seems to have met with universal acceptance in the embossed fancy tableware is the "Beehive" offered in various styles of colouring.'

However, an invoice addressed to 'The Controller & Treasurer to Her Majesty Queen Mary, Buckingham Palace, London' shows that the Queen ordered 12 Beehive teapots in size No. 10 (in natural colours), with the order being dated for the 15th July 1936 and the invoice dated for the 19th September 1936.

The design consists of a domed beehive shape, rather unrealistically decorated with flowers in pastel shades. Where there is a finial, it consists of a bee with folded wings. The most commonly seen colour is a light tan with the base of the piece, as in a cruet, represented as vivid green green grass bordered by a small brown fence.

The teapot is of a rather squat appearance, while biscuit barrels have been found in both a squat and tall shape. Butter and cheese dishes have a square or oblong base in cream bordered with green; occasionally, a chromium plate base was supplied.

Primrose, which can sometimes appear to be a pale cream, was offered as an alternative colourway. Rather more rarely found today, is the pale blue colourway. Sugar shakers can also be found with the upper part in the tan colourway with the base in a greyish lavender.

The dessert plate shows a colourful scene with three tan beehives set next to a branching tree. A flagged path leads to a half-seen cottage, fronted by tall pink hollyhocks.

H.M. Queen Mary was obviously impressed with the Beehive design as, in February 1937, she placed a further order for '6 each of covered butters, cheeses, teapots, cruets (3 piece), and honies (with fast stands)'. These were all listed against the pattern number 3284.

Items found today are biscuit barrels with wicker work handles, tea pots with matching cream jugs and sugar bowls, butter dishes, cruet and condiment sets, cheese dishes, dessert plates (more popularly used as wall plates today) preserve pots (some with fast stands, some without), sugar shakers, and chargers (large plates intended for wall hanging).

'Castle on the Hill'   (picture page 56)

Date of manufacture 1930s+
Backstamp 6 with REGISTRATION APPLIED FOR

So far, this pattern has been found only as the illustrated cheese dish, and carries no pattern name. The cover is modelled as a hill with a castle perched on top. The building is picked out in tan and orange, and green foliage partially covers the walls. A stepped path leads down to a gated fence which is interspersed with trees. The base of the cheese dish has a green grassy border with a path at either end.

Chanticleer   (picture page 56, 57)

Date of manufacture 1936+
Registered numbers 810173 and 810775
Backstamp 7, 11, 13, 14, 19, 29, 30

Cockerels and hens have always been popular additions to the breakfast table and Chanticleer was no exception. Realistically moulded in warm colours, the cock and his hen were classed as 'distinctive novelties' in the Grimwades advertising leaflets. The range first went on show at the British Industries Fair in February 1936, along with Lakeland and Pixie.

With the exception of the toast rack, the items produced were in the shape of the bird set on a grassy green base. They were available in different colourways, with the hand painting adding variations to these. The teapot, for example, can be found in streaked and speckled shades of a golden brown, with the tail and lower body feathers highlighted in soft green. Alternatively, a rich, dark blue combination was used with bands of scarlet emphasising the tail feathers. These tail feathers curve down to create the handle of the tea pot, with the spout being formed by the open beak of the bird. Sugar shakers were either golden brown or a pale yellow lightly streaked with red, the wings being a light grey and the breast cream.

What appears to be a cock bird set in a nesting pose was modelled for the cover of a cheese dish. A cream colourway was used in combination with dark grey for the breast and tail feathers.

Toast racks are in green with a cockerel decorating either end; 3-piece cruets (salt and pepper pots on a base) show the cockerel standing with his head held high, while the hen stares into space. The 4-piece condiment set (salt, pepper and covered mustard pot on a base) has the cockerel in the same proud pose, accompanied by two hens, one as before, the other shown head down, pecking for food. The male bird always sports a large scarlet comb and scarlet wattle, while the hen has only the merest suggestion of a comb. The base resembles a grassy field, the carrying handle depicting a fence.

Items listed in the trade catalogue were 'teapot, hot water jug, sugar and cream, marmalade with cover, sugar sifter, cheese cover and stand, Cruet

(3 pieces), condiment set (4 pieces). 3-bar toast rack, 5-bar toast rack, jam, covered butter, mint boat and stand, dessert plate.' In addition to this published list, a milk jug has also been found.

Some items bear the name Chanticleer (which is French for cockerel), while others are marked Rooster. The former would appear to apply to the golden brown colourway, the latter to the blue colourway. Both names carry the same registered number. Occasionally, items are marked only with the backstamp, but on small items such as sugar shakers, and cruets and/or condiments sets, this can be missing altogether.

Countryside   (picture page 57)

Date of manufacture 1938
Backstamp 31

Like 'Castle on the Hill', very few pieces, other than the one illustrated, have been found. The dish shows an orange-roofed water mill set on a slight hill beside a rushing river. A stepped, winding path leads to a small bridge over the water.

The pattern was mentioned in the trade papers in October 1938, when it was exhibited at the trade fair at Olympia, although it was erroneously described as portraying a windmill rather than a water mill. In 1939, H.M. Queen Mary ordered 6 open trays in the Countryside pattern at a cost of 1/- (5p) each.

Crocus   (picture page 57)

Date of manufacture 1930s+
Backstamp 32

The Crocus pattern falls into two categories: Relief Moulded Ware and Pastels (see chapter on Pastels). As a sundae dish, attractively hand painted in shades of pink, green and yellow, it is definitely relief moulded ware. However, other wares made in the same series have a highly glazed pastel body with only the flower shown in relief. The pastel shades are invariably green with the crocus itself portrayed in varying colours.

A range of table ware was produced, although the complete list is not known.

'Dovecote'   (picture page 58)

Date of manufacture 1936
Backstamp 1,7

Although illustrated in *The Pottery Gazette* in September 1936, this design was not actually named in the advertising so the title 'Dovecote' has been used for identification purposes only, for the ease of collectors.

The range would appear to consist more of decorative items rather than table ware with fruit bowls and flower vases of various shapes and sizes being made. Items were made with both a matt and gloss glaze. The matt example shows a dovecote modelled in relief with brightly coloured flowers surrounding it. Grey-blue doves flock around. The ground colour is cream. The gloss example is less well-modelled and the hand-painting is less well-defined. This would suggest a later date of manufacture.

'Galleon' (picture page 58)

Date of manufacture 1930s
Backstamp 9

The biscuit box shown appears to have been modelled on an Elizabethan galleon, and sails on a painted sea. An animal is used for the figurehead and, at the stern, high windows are picked out in blue. The planked body of the ship is brown, with the gun ports emphasised with black and orange. The knob or finial consists of a cut-out metal galleon but it is not known whether this is original to the piece, or a later replacement by a loving owner. Unfortunately, the design bears no name.

Game (picture page 58)

Date of manufacture 1936
Backstamp 9

A photograph for this series appeared in the trade papers in September 1936, advertising it as suitable for gift ware.

The series shows a mallard in flight over a lake fringed with irises. It was made in two colourways. In one, the bird can be seen painted predominantly in shades of lilac, set against a cream ground; the irises are tinged with blue. This cream colourway is more rarely found than the dark blue.

The dark blue colourway has the bird, brightly coloured, flying across clouds outlined in gilt. The foreground is also very colourful, the irises being hand painted in yellow, pink and blue.

Gera (picture page 59, 60)

Date of manufacture 1934
Registered number 797640. Registered Canada 1934
Pattern number 2209
Backstamp 6, 33

Gera, a flower-embossed design, is very pretty and appealing. The Grimwades trade catalogue describes it as, 'A most attractive adaptation in strong relief of the popular Geranium Foliage and Flower in natural colours with an appropriate rustic background. This design is made in three distinct colourings.'

A later catalogue describes it as 'A new series of table ware having for its special motif a well-modelled spray of Geranium flower and foliage in strong relief with wicker work background in low relief. This affords great scope for very tasteful and effective decorations. Made in six distinct varieties.'

More information can be gleaned from the January 1934 edition of *The Pottery Gazette*. 'Another new suite that is being prepared for the New Year trade is the "Gera". The decoration of this is based upon the geranium, and the arrangement of the design consists of a series of geranium sprays which spring from variegated foliage at the base. This pattern, like the "Regina" will lend itself to various styles of treatment, from natural to conventional. One very simple way in which the new "Gera" ware will be offered will be in the plain old ivory style, without any added colouring. All that will happen will be that the embossment will be allowed to appear a little whiter than the brownish-tinted glaze. We feel quite sure that ware of this type, simple and unassuming though it may be, will command attention on other grounds than that it will be relatively inexpensive.'

A further account, which gives us some clues as to the colours in which Gera was available, was published by the same periodical in January 1935, '... the ware is dealt with first of all in a basic ground colour – which may be bright green, Wedgwood blue, or a delicate shade of fawn – and the floral work is over-pencilled (i.e. over-painted) in colour, the leafage being naturally tinted and the flowers left in low relief. Alternatively, the pattern can be had with an ivory ground, in which case the geranium is emphasised naturalistically in red or pink.'

In fact, a more dramatic colourway was also issued, with the flowers painted a vivid scarlet against a black ground.

Items available at the time were listed by Grimwades as: Tea pots, tea pot stands, cream and sugar sets, jugs (5 sizes), marmalade pots, butter dishes with stands, cheese dishes, covered milk or hot water jugs, 3- and 5-bar toast racks, salad bowls (with servers), condiment sets on trays, dessert plates, 3-compartment and twin-compartment trays, sweet dishes, sandwich sets, cups, saucers and tea plates, sugar sifters, mint boats and stands, and comports or cake plates with integral stands.

The pattern name is also used as the name for the shape and pieces can be found bearing GERA impressed on the base.

'Grapes'

(picture page 60)

Date of manufacture 1934+
Backstamp 7

Like the 'Apple' design, this has been found only as a preserve pot. The body of the pot, with its integral base, is made up from vine leaves hand painted in shades of yellow, green and pink, with a few grapes scattered about. The lid consists of grapes painted a purplish blue, the knob or finial being formed by the stalk of the vine leaf.

'Haystack'

(picture page 60)

Date of manufacture 1934+
Backstamp 6

It is possible that the teapot illustrated is part of the Chanticleer/Rooster series as the finial of the lid portrays a cockerel. However, as no haystacks are depicted in Chanticleer, this design has been given a separate entry. The body of the teapot is formed as an old-fashioned round haystack, tapering to the base which is surrounded by a wattle fence interspersed with colourful flowers. The handle is formed by a tree in full leaf.

'Iris'   (picture page 61)

Date of manufacture 1934+
Backstamp 6

The only known example of this is a tall jug, the body formed of overlapping iris leaves, with the purple flowers arranged in a deep band around the rim. The jug was reproduced in the 1950s/1960s, but the modelling was less sharp, and the colours of pale pink and pale blue seeming dull and unattractive.

Lakeland   (picture page 61, 62)

Date of manufacture 1936
Registered number 810588
Pattern number 3015
Backstamp 34, 35

The Lakeland series was first mentioned in the trade papers in February 1936 with Grimwades taking out a full page advertisement. The ware would be seen, stated the advertisement, at the British Industries Fair which was taking place that month. Also introduced were the series Chanticleer and Pixie.

In March 1937, H.M. Queen Mary placed an order for 6 plates No. 20 at a cost of 1/4d (about 7p) each. She also ordered a salad bowl and servers, No. 19 and 19A at 4/6d (22¹/₂p).

The design takes two forms, the main one portraying a lakeside scene, flanked on one side by trees, with a range of hills beyond. The other portrayal seems to have been used only on flower holders. These were modelled in the shape of tree trunks with three or four apertures at the top to take the flowers. Leaves and flowers decorate the trunks and a large butterfly is prominent. Colours of the trunk are brown, the foliage green, although a different colourway is provided with a lilac trunk and yellow foliage.

Two colourways were used for other items. The most frequently found uses a green palette for the grass, trees and shrubs, with flowers being picked out in pink. The alternative has green grass, yellow foliage, and yellow and lilac flowers. In addition, the hills and lake are tinged with lilac.

Items made include teapots, cream and sugar sets, hot water jugs, milk jugs, compartmented dishes, preserve pots, mint boats and stands, sugar shakers, coffee pots and so on.

Lotus   (picture page57)

Date of manufacture 1934+
Backstamp 6

To date, this has been found only as a lidded preserve pot. The base is attractively shaped from leaves and hand painted in blue. The lid shows the expanded flower in yellow with a lily bud as the knob or finial. The base is impressed with the shape name Lotus.

'Pagoda' (picture page 63)

Date of manufacture 1934+
Backstamp 6

This has been named from the mustard pot in the condiment set which is shaped like a small wooden pagoda. The roof is picked out in orange and the salt and pepper pots are shaped like bushes planted in wooden tubs. The base consists of a paved garden. The orange roof features again in the toastrack and is seen atop a wooden gate. The sugar sifter, in the shape of a water pump, and the twin-compartment dish have also been included in this pattern, as both feature distinctive similarities.

Peony (picture page 63)

Date of manufacture 1938
Backstamp 6

An extremely pretty range of tableware, Peony, was introduced in 1938 and was illustrated as a new suite of tableware in the trade papers in October of that year. It is possible that the production run was short-lived due to the impending war as very few pieces of this pattern have been found.

The muffin dish illustrated has a plain cream base, bordered by green leaves while the cover is formed of cream petals, shading to a deep pink at the edges, with a touch of blue at the base. The knob or finial is composed of the flower, set on a leaf and accompanied by yellow and pink stamens. A yellow colourway was also used, but the modelling is not as crisp, the glaze glossier and the hand painting less well done.

Peony was issued in teapots, cream and sugar sets, cups and saucers, preserve pots, cheese and muffin dishes, serving and triple dishes, condiment set, sugar shakers and toast racks.

Pixie (picture page 63, 64)

Date of manufacture 1936
Registered numbers 811696 and 811804
Pattern number 4037
Backstamp 6, 11, 13, 36

Pixie was introduced in 1936, along with Lakeland and Chanticleer, and was mentioned by *The Trade Gazette* in its February issue when it was written, 'Good business is confidently expected with these new lines.'

H.M. Queen Mary was obviously impressed, as an order from Marlborough House in March 1937 lists a request for teapots, hot water jugs, cheese dishes and cruets.

There would appear to be three different colour treatments of the Pixie pattern; the scenes, however, are all similar. The latest made is the one hand painted in pastel colours. A reclining pixie is seen relaxing on the grass in front of a garden wall. He is set against a background of toadstools, and shaded by a tree bearing bunches of cherries. The pixie is also seen standing and kneeling, and in the dessert plates, two pixies can be found relaxing by the side of a lake, with one playing a musical instrument. A frog is shown in the foreground of the large jug, but has not been seen on any of the other pieces.

In the pastel shades, both the fruit and the toadstools are painted in various colours of pink, yellow, blue and lilac. The pixie is dressed in either yellow with a blue cap or blue with a yellow cap and these are all marked with Backstamp 13. Where the pixie is shown wearing bright red clothes, the backstamp is either Backstamp 6, 11 or 36 – all appear to have been used. A jam pot has been found without pixies; only the cherry tree with its fruit is portrayed.

Items bearing Backstamp 6 come in a choice of two colourways. The first shows the pixie wearing a dark red outfit; the wall is tan and the cherries are purple. In the second, the pixie wears mid- to dark green, the wall is lilac and the fruit is a bright orangey red. The toadstools in both are yellow tinged with red.

A possible fourth colourway depicts a pixie dressed in black with a blue hat. The toadstools are very pale and in yellow and blue. The grass is pale green. It is not known whether this rather drab colourway ever went into full production.

Primula

(picture page 65, 66)

Date of manufacture 1933+ and 1934+
Pattern numbers 1802, 1847, 1848, 4667, 4668, 4669, 4715
Backstamp 6, 37, 38

Based on the flower, Primula was first manufactured in 1933 with a different colourway appearing in 1934. It can be found bearing either the Royal Winton backstamp or the Rubian Art backstamp.

The Pottery Trade Gazette wrote, 'Grimwades Ltd are embarking upon a new rendition of their now everywhere well-known "Primula" ware. It will in future be featured as an alternative to the older style, in old ivory with floral sprays treated in natural colours. It will be conceded everywhere that the "Primula" ware has been a great success during 1933, and when we announce that it is now being reintroduced in an entirely new treatment, which is generally acknowledged by all who have seen the preliminary pieces even to surpass the original, there is not likely to be much doubt that fresh interest will be aroused in it.'

A Grimwades catalogue sheet for 1933 shows four varieties of the ware, all set against green foliage and each having a different pattern number: with mauve flowers (4667), with cardinal red flowers (4668), with yellow flowers (4669) and with pink flowers (4715).

Another catalogue sheet extols later ware. 'The treatment of this popular subject provides a contrast to the purely natural (i.e. the green foliage), as the foliage background is in rich old ivory with delicate hand tracing in brown, thus emphasising the rich colouring of the flowers in a very striking manner.' This later ware was made in three varieties, all set on the ivory ground. The catalogue went on, 'delicate blue flowers (1802), cardinal red flowers (1847) and sweet pink flowers (1848)'. Another alternative shows pale green and cream leaves, with flowers in shades of pink, mauve and yellow.

These catalogue pages also list items of tableware in Primula series made by Atlas China, a subsidiary company owned by Grimwades, but to date no pieces have been found.

In February 1939, a Grimwades' invoice shows that H.M. Queen Mary ordered 6 teapots and 6 large jugs in Primula and these cost 2/- (10p) and 1/9 (8³/₄p) respectively. The items were identified by the number 5114 and it is possible that the number applies to the colourway having pale green and cream leaves, with flowers in shades of pink, mauve and yellow, mentioned above.

The list of items manufactured seems endless, sweet dishes, sugar sifters, cruets, condiment sets, covered jugs, egg sets, 3- and 5-bar toast racks, triple trays, marmalade pots, cheese dishes (2 sizes), mint boats and stands, teapots (2 sizes), dessert plates, cream and sugar sets, 7-piece dessert sets, cake comports, sandwich trays and plates, salad bowls, and sets of jugs.

Regina (picture page 66)

Date of manufacture 1934
Backstamp 39

Based on the Regina water lily, the series features the flower resting on its large leaves. It was introduced by Grimwades in February 1934, 'Amongst the many new novelties for 1934, the new "Regina" suite is strongly recommended. It depicts a choice study of the Water Lily on strongly modelled embossed Ivory Ware. Made in various colouring, Warm Brown, Blue-Grey, Green, and Mauve.'

The trade press echoed the manufacturers, 'This new ware is ... relief embossed, and in shape alone it is of such ornamental value that it is quite attractive without any decoration other than the merest ground tinting. It has, therefore, been decided by the firm to give the pattern a run in this way, as a simple decorative suite to be offered in four principal ground colours, green, old gold, mauve and pale blue ... if however, he (the dealer) should require something more elaborate, he will find on the same shape a number of renderings which involve the picking-in of the leafage and foliage embossment with strong colourings.'

Pieces having green foliage can be found in the two distinct varieties mentioned above. The pastel green has flowers in pale creamy yellow, and could be regarded as more attractive than the stronger green version which has the flowers enhanced with strokes of orange.

Like Primula, Regina was made in a wide range of tableware and Grimwades list articles such as footed salad bowls, sets of jugs, teapots and stands, hot water jugs, cheese dishes, 2- and 3- piece cruets, 3- and 5-bar toast racks, honey pots, sugar sifters, dessert plates, triple trays, watercress dishes and stands, mint boats and stands, sweet dishes, chocolate comports, handled cake stands, footed fruit or cake stands, tea cups and saucers, tea plates, sugar and cream sets.

Rooster – See Chanticleer

'Salad' (picture page 66)

Date of manufacture 1930s
Backstamp 1, 6

Introduced in 1930 and advertised by Grimwades during that period, the ware initially consisted of 'a range of salad, cucumber and cress ware, decorated with green leafage and red tomatoes.'

A page from a contemporary Grimwades catalogue for the 1930s shows an elongated celery tray 'in natural colours' and a similar rhubarb dish 'in natural pink and green'. A round dish, 'Savoy' depicted a cabbage leaf, while a biscuit box was made, rather strangely, in the shape of a rough-skinned melon. Salad and fruit bowls were made in both 'Tomato Salad' and 'Vine', the latter covered in grapes and vine leaves. In keeping with the natural theme, flower pots were made which resembled wicker baskets.

A worker at Grimwades at the time maintains that some of the salad ware, such as 'an open lettuce leaf dish' was marketed under the name of Middleton ware, and was mentioned in a gardening programme on the radio during the late 1930s.

Later production included dishes decorated with green pea pods, turnips, radishes, spring onions and rather improbable carrots, all set against a vivid green ground.

However, the idea of making salad and vegetable tableware was not a new one, as a rhubarb dish was introduced in 1900. The dish, realistically portrayed, was intended for stewed rhubarb. A tomato dish also made its appearance at this time, as well as an elongated lettuce dish (available in 4 sizes), in natural colouring. In 1901, a lettuce cheese dish and cover was advertised, together with a leaf-moulded bowl intended for punch or junket.

Terrace (picture page 67)

Date of manufacture 1937+
Pattern number 4094
Backstamp 6

This was initially advertised in October 1937 when the trade papers wrote, 'There are also many excellent lines in matt-glazed ware, of which the "Terrace" pattern may be cited as typical.' Pieces can also be found with a high-gloss glaze, however.

The scene depicted shows a stepped path, flanked by brightly coloured garden flowers, leading up to a balustraded terrace. Leafy green trees set against a creamy white form the background. This creamy white is sometimes subtly shaded with pale lavender. The body of the piece is also slightly unevenly ribbed. Pieces made include wall chargers, and ornamental jugs and vases of various forms.

A different colourway is used for both the high-gloss dessert plate and the condiment set and is of soft beiges and browns, with the flowers picked out in more subdued colours.

Trellis Rose Garden

(picture page 68)

Date of manufacture 1938
Backstamp 6

Perhaps one of the prettiest designs in relief moulded ware, Trellis Rose Garden was mentioned in *The Pottery Gazette* in February 1938. The trade paper was previewing exhibits to be shown at the British Trade Fair. `A new series of relief modelled wares is in the course of preparation, to be known as "Trellis Rose Garden". Whether the modelling of the whole of the pieces will have been completed by the time the Fair opens is a moot point, for a good deal is entailed in its preparation, but there will be a sufficiency of samples on view to show what the entire suite, when finished, will be like.'

The *Gazette* was correct in its comments; Trellis Rose Garden is perhaps the most detailed pattern of all the relief moulded ware, consisting, as it does, of rustic trellis complete with rambling roses in pink and yellow. The flowers and leaves are finely modelled and delicately painted. Between the trellis, on larger pieces, can be caught a glimpse of an extended English garden complete with a brick wall and crazy paving.

There is no list available of exactly what the suite comprised but a safe guess would be table ware, as in most of the other ranges.

'Wishing Well'

(picture page 54)

Date of manufacture 1950s
Backstamp 14

The jam pot illustrated is the only known example of this design. It features an attractive, covered well, the base of which is decorated with foxgloves and other flowers. The lid forms the cover of the well and is complete with winding chain.

Pastels

The popular pastel series made its first appearance in 1940 and was hailed enthusiastically by the trade press in April of that year.

Rosebud was the first design made and *The Pottery Gazette* described it so, 'Another attractive but inexpensive line is offered in air-blown colourings *beneath the glaze*, with the handles and knobs of the hollow pieces formed by means of a delicately modelled rosebud, which is coloured up naturally by brushwork.'

Huge amounts were made specifically for export – only undecorated white ware was allowed to be manufactured for the home market during, and shortly after, the war years – and it was initially exported to Canada, Australia, New Zealand, India and South Africa, being exported to America later.

The trade papers listed the items available in Rosebud as: morning sets, coffee sets, afternoon sets (which would include a teapot), chocolate comports, covered honey pots, cheese dishes, butter trays and knives, jugs (in 5 sizes), open trays, salad bowls and servers, hot water jugs, sweet dishes, cruets, toast racks, watercress dishes, triple trays and bedside sets.

By the 1950s, the range had been extended to include dinner ware as well. Wall pockets can be found in some designs, such as Petunia, Rosebud and Tea Rose, while dressing table and trinket sets were also produced.

Items of Rosebud were sometimes impressed with the pattern name and some Rosebud shapes were not exclusive to the range. The Thistle jam pot carries the name, and collectors can also find chintz-decorated pieces impressed ROSEBUD. Petunia and Honey Lily shapes were also used for chintz patterns.

Pastel ware was occasionally manufactured without the flowers being hand-painted. These were issued in a plain colour or with the flower shown in white; the ground colour was usually green. Some patterns, such as Petunia were highlighted with gilding, rather than being hand painted in natural colours.

The glaze used on the Pastels seems particularly prone to age and fine glazings cracks are frequently found. The cracks are on the surface only, but can sometimes spoil the look of the piece.

'Apple'
(picture page 69)

Date of manufacture 1950s
Backstamp 13

An Apple design also appears in the Relief Moulded Ware chapter. However, that was made in the 1930s and bears little resemblance to the Apple illustrated in the Relief Moulded section.

The fruit is shown in relief against a pale green ground and reflects autumnal colours. It has also been seen on an amber ground.

'Apple Blossom' (picture page 69)

Date of manufacture 1950s
Backstamp 13

The low fruit or dessert bowl is a warm pale green with the blossom shown in relief in pink and white. Like Apple (above), it does not appear to have been made extensively. It has also been seen with pale blue and pale pink ground colours.

Briar (picture page 69)

Date of manufacture 1940s
Backstamp 7, 40

Featuring the flower of the Briar Rose, this pattern was available in two colourways, green or cream. The cream ground is enhanced by the flowers hand painted in yellow, blue and pink, while the green colourway is rather duller with flowers in old gold, tan and blue. Very little actual tableware is to be found, leading one to think that it was less successful than some of the other patterns.

Crocus (picture page 57)

Date of manufacture 1930s+
Backstamp 32

The Crocus pattern falls into two categories: Relief Moulded Ware and Pastels. It has, therefore been included in both the Pastels chapter and the Relief Moulded Ware chapter. A range of table ware was produced although the complete list is not known.

The sundae dish illustrated is attractively hand painted in shades of pink, green and yellow, and is classed as relief moulded ware. However, other wares made in the same series have a highly glazed pastel body with only the flower shown in relief. The pastel shades are invariably green with the crocus itself portrayed in varying colours, as in the sugar shaker illustrated.

Fuchsia (picture page 69)

Date of manufacture 1950s+
Backstamp 12, 13, 17

The flower is naturalistically depicted against the plain ground colours which came in a choice of pale blue, pale green, yellow and pink. Like Briar (above), it does not appear to have been made in any great quantity.

Hibiscus (picture page 70)

Date of manufacture 1950s+
Backstamp 7, 13

This pattern can easily be confused with that of Honey Lily (Tiger Lily) as the modelling is identical. However, the Hibiscus flower is portrayed in pale pink, shading to dark pink, and is quite plain, having no streaking or mottling on the petals. Hibiscus was targeted specifically at the American market and is found less often in this country.

Honey Lily
(picture page 70)

Date of manufacture 1950s+
Pattern numbers 5774 (green), 5777 (cream with striped border), 5803 (could be 5802) yellow
Backstamp 7, 11, 13, 14, 41

Known to many collectors as Tiger Lily, the Honey Lily pattern was made mainly in sunshine yellow and a soft green. More rarely seen is the cream colourway which has a banded border of green and pink.

The flower, like the Fuchsia pattern, is well modelled and stands out in relief. It closely resembles Hibiscus, and the company appear to have used the same moulds. The Honey lily flower, however, has mottling on the petals which are absent on Hibiscus. The Honey Lily flowers are also lightly streaked with yellow, whereas the Hibiscus is solid pink.

Table ware was made, possibly on the scale of that of Rosebud, but unfortunately records are not available to verify this.

Mottled and Plain Coloured Ware
(picture page 75)

Date of manufacture 1939+
Backstamp 7, 14

Wares made in plain and mottled finishes were produced during the war years and the 'Buyers' Notes' in *The Pottery Gazette* dated October 1939 mentions 'several ranges of teaware in mottled self-colourings underglaze. The principal colours are pink, green, primrose, grey and amber; the finish is gold edge and half-solid handle.'

In addition to the tableware, the mottled ware included lamp bases, vases and wall pockets. It was also occasionally used on some of the flower patterns (see Fuchsia illustration). Clocks were made in plain, shaded colours.

Pansy
(picture page 71)

Date of manufacture 1940s+
Backstamp 11, 13, 14

This is a very simplistic pattern, featuring the garden flower, which is moulded in relief and emphasised by handpainting. Larger items have the flower accompanied by its foliage while smaller items, such as the ashtray illustrated, consist solely of the flower-head. It's not a pattern which is seen often and it is extremely pretty, especially when the stronger blue and mauve colours are used for the flowers, although the vivid yellow flowers contrast well with the pale green ground, as seen on the hors d'oeuvre dish.

There is no record of the amount of Pansy that was produced but, as it is seldom seen in the market place, it would appear to have been of limited production. Neither is it known if any tableware was made.

Petunia
(picture page 71)

Date of manufacture 1940s+
Pattern numbers 405 (pink), 466 (yellow)
Backstamp 11, 12, 13, 42

Petunia ware was made in pink, yellow and mottled pink. This pattern is extremely popular with collectors and is, indeed, most attractive. The flower is depicted in white with a deep pink centre and is enhanced by green leaves. In some pieces the pink centre is omitted, leaving the flower plain white. Occasionally, the flower is highlighted with gilding.

Apart from tableware, vases were made, as well as items for the dressing table. The name PETUNIA is occasionally impressed on the base of the piece.

Rosebud
(picture page 72, 73, 74)

Date of manufacture 1940s+
Pattern numbers 5488 (yellow), 5489 (green), 5490 (pink). The number 44 has been found on a cream ground cup.
Backstamp 7, 11, 12, 13, 14

Rosebud is, perhaps, the most popular pattern with collectors and is quite readily available. It was first produced in the 1940s and was greatly admired by the trade (see the introductory paragraphs to Pastels).

The flower is depicted as a half-open pink bud, accompanied by green leaves lightly streaked with yellow. It is used as a finial (knob) for tea and coffee pots etc, and forms the feet of salad bowls. Salt and pepper pots are shaped as rosebuds and are set on a plain green leaf-shaped base. The only time the flower has been seen in full bloom (similar to Tea Rose) is on the sugar shaker which carries the pattern number 5489 – a Rosebud pattern number.

The Rosebud pattern was in production for many years and an advertisement was inserted in the American *Crockery and Glass Trade Journal* in October 1952 by the Ebeling & Reuss Company, who featured the range, announcing the arrival of 'Rosebud' Royal Winton, imported from England. They went on to state, 'Ebeling & Reuss Co., is proud to announce that they have been appointed exclusive US Distributors of this very well known line, featuring *embossed* rosebuds as the decorative motif. The line is available in three pastel colours: green, rose or yellow, edged in gold. Not only does the line include dinnerware, but features a handsome and unique group of matching accessories.'

The American advertisement goes on to list the items available as table and dinner ware, teapot stands, oval platters, double egg cups, round bonbons, 7-piece bedside sets, covered cheese dishes, tennis sets, Jumbo cups and saucers, butter dishes (with knife), chop plates, and covered toasts (*sic*).

At some point, a small amount of cream coloured Rosebud was made, but to date, very little has been found in this colourway.

The ware is often impressed with the name ROSEBUD beneath.

'Tea Rose'
(picture page 74)

Date of manufacture 1940s+
Backstamp 11, 13, 14

This is impossible to confuse with Rosebud as the rose shown is in full bloom. It is rarely found and so far, has appeared in three colours, on a pale blue-green ground, a pale primrose ground and a pink ground. The flower is particularly well-modelled and is predominantly pink with yellow shading. The leaves are arranged in a spray and are accompanied by rosebuds. As the flower seems to take up so much space on the piece, it is possible that it was reserved for ornamental items only, rather than more practical tableware.

'Thistle'
(picture page 75)

Date of manufacture 1950s
Backstamp 14

The Thistle pattern shows the flower in streaked purple and green and it is used as a finial on jam pots. Showing an economy of design, Grimwades used a Rosebud body for the jam pot and the name is impressed into the base. The candlestick uses the flower for the nozzle.

'Tiger Lily' – see Honey Lily

Hand Painted Ware

Although the relief-moulded and pastel ware benefited from having the raised detail hand painted, Grimwades did issue several items that were hand painted in an entirely different manner and which were often signed by the artist.

These ranges differ enormously in style. The first to be manufactured was the Art Deco series painted in vivid flamboyant colours (see chapter on Art Deco) which was introduced in 1930.

The second range was produced in the mid-1930s when romantic scenery was portrayed in soft pastel colours (see Garden Scenes below). Some of these hand painted patterns were later transferred on to lithographs and issued in quantity.

The third range appeared in 1940 with items being decorated with groups of flowers, fruit or game birds (see Flowers and Fruit below).

With precious records being destroyed, it has proved impossible to identify the artists who initialled their work or to expand upon the lives of those who signed their pieces. Perhaps more information will come to light as more research is carried out.

GARDEN SCENES
Delphiniums   (picture page 76)
Date of manufacture 1936
Backstamp 43

In 1936, H.M. Queen Mary placed an order for a 'Dish Hand Painted No. 7 (14 inch plaque Garden Scene)' and another for 'Dish Hand Painted No. 8 (Bowl Arosa. Delphiniums)' of which samples were retained by the company. It is highly likely that the pattern Delphiniums is the one illustrated on page 76. The bowl is signed W.H. and features a stepped bridge that spans a lake or river. A rose arbour is shown at the centre of the bridge, with poplars behind. In the foreground are clumps of blue delphiniums flanked by bushes of yellow flowers tinged with red.

'Galleon'   (picture page 76)
Date of manufacture 1950s
Backstamp 17

Hand painting continued well into the 1950s when the table lamp featuring a galleon was made. The stylised Elizabethan sailing ship is picked out in pale yet definite pastel colours, while the background is softly dappled.

'Poplars' (picture page 76)

Date of manufacture mid-1930s
Backstamp 6

The pattern on the jug could be the one referred to as Garden Scene in the Grimwades' invoice but it is impossible to be certain. The jug bears the signature H.C. Lea and depicts banks of flowers set beside an urn which is placed on a tall plinth. The other side of the jug features a glimpse of a lake, and the whole is set against a background of poplar trees.

Red Roof (picture page 76)

Date of manufacture 1930s
Backstamp 44

Although not strictly a garden scene, the Red Roof pattern is worthy of inclusion in the hand painted chapter. Known also to collectors as Red Roof Cottage, it shows a view of houses or cottages nestling against the hillside, with a stretch of water and grass in front. The ground colour is a deep cream, almost yellow, which contrasts well with the green of the poplar trees. The houses consist of simple black outlines with the roofs hand painted in blocks of vivid red. The distant hills are blue and blue brush-strokes indicate the sky.

There is another similar pattern which is transfer printed and which is known to collectors as Red Roof Cottage with Pond. It is possibly a more romantic and detailed version of Red Roof, and shows a timber-framed house with a red roof set in front of a group of trees. In front is a river (or pond) which flows beneath a white-fenced bridge. The foreground is composed of numerous wild flowers and the ground colour is cream.

'6742' (picture page 77)

Date of manufacture mid-1930s
Backstamp 6, 9, 45, 46

Trees are also prominent in this design. Willows overhang a curving stone bridge while the foreground is brightened with a mass of brightly coloured crocus.

The large shallow bowl is signed F Phillips and the pattern was later transfer printed for mass production. The plate and biscuit barrel are transfer printed with the pattern number '6742' in blue. It is probable that the pattern was used on a range of tableware, although few items have been found so far.

FLOWERS AND FRUIT

The Anemone pattern is perhaps the most popular and most frequently found of the flower and fruit designs. It was first produced in the 1940s and was initially issued for export only. The pattern was described in November 1940 by *The Pottery Gazette* as, 'The pieces...are much more than ordinarily interesting. The decoration is quite a new one and features anemones arranged upon a mossy background after the style of the pictorial work which came so freely and skilfully from the brush of the famous still-life painter – Wm. Hunt – who used to paint in pure water colour on a basis of white, thus achieving a brilliance which has never been excelled. The "Anemone" decoration is appealing and we feel sure it will be successful; in fact, we are assured the pattern has already proved a certain seller.'

After World War II, a team of three Polish refugees was employed by Grimwades on a piece work basis. Philip Plant, grandson to James Plant, identifies the signature Z. Kas, sometimes seen on the Anemone pattern, as belonging to one of the Polish workers. He was rumoured to be a former Polish ambassador to Lebanon and a High Court judge. He apparently lived in the Polish camp at Stafford and commuted to Stoke daily by train. It is thought his surname was Kojzinsky (*sic*).

Anemone

Date of manufacture 1940
Pattern number 5633
Backstamp 14

The anemones are seen grouped against a soft amber ground, shaded here and there with apricot and ochre. The flowers are in cerise, rust, white and blue; the leaves a soft green. The background is hand painted, the anemones transfer printed.

'Roses'

Date of manufacture 1940s
Backstamp 13

Full blown and budding tea roses are shown in this pattern. The background is hand painted and executed in a range of soft autumnal colours. The transfer printed roses are in shades of red, and pale and deep pink, with a single yellow rose and bud included. Some of these pieces were signed b. Austin.

'Fruit'

Date of manufacture 1940s-60s
Backstamp 13, 18

The basket (illustrated) would appear to be entirely hand painted with no transfer printing, as is seen on Anemone and Roses. It could therefore be a prototype which later went into production. The ground colour is shaded, like the flower designs, with the fruits being portrayed in a naturalistic fashion. Strawberries, grapes and tiny gooseberries feature on one side of the piece, with pears, cherries and blackberries on the other. It was made in the early 1940s.

The pattern on the jug (illustrated) was completely transfer printed. The pattern consists of large rounded apples, accompanied by gooseberries and shiny blackcurrants and has a very autumnal colouring. It is signed J. Birbek with the figure 25 below. However, the base of the jug bears the hand painted mark NOJ/54 with a black transfer printed backstamp (Backstamp 18) which was still being used, with refinements in the 1990s. However, it is more likely that the jug dates from the 1950s and that NOJ/54 is a year mark.

'Game Birds'

(picture page 78)

Date of manufacture 1940s
Backstamp 12 with COMOY'S OF LONDON curved above.

This is more work by b. Austin, with the background colours being hand painted and the game birds transfer printed. The pheasants are finely drawn, the cock resplendently coloured, the hen more drab. On the reverse of the piece, a pair of male and female woodcock are featured. It is interesting to note that a colour page from a 1917/1918 catalogue shows vases decorated with game birds almost identical to the ones seen on the tobacco jar.

Art Deco

With the advent of Art Deco in the 1920s, it was only natural for Grimwades to follow suit and produce their own designs. The majority were hand painted, although some, such as 'Jazz' and 'Jigsaw' were transfer printed. The ware was issued under both the Royal Winton and Rubian Art trade names. However, like everything else produced by Grimwades from about 1928, there is little or no documentation and tantalising questions have to remain unanswered.

The Pottery Gazette for November 1930 states briefly, that 'Persian ware, No. 9882, in fully fledged colouring, is also worthy of recommendation.' A poor and rather grainy black and white photographic reproduction on the same page shows a range of ware in geometric designs. The photograph also shows the new Delhi pattern. Apart from that, there is no other reference to the new and exciting products.

Some of the ware was hand painted while some was transfer printed, with the designs being used on vases, bowls, candy boxes, comports and so on, as well as table ware.

'Blocks' (picture page 79)

Date of manufacture 1930s
Backstamp 5

Blocks of colour are set against a white ground and arranged in rows, broken only by stepped blocks of black, together with black and white zigzags. The colours are less vivid than on other Art Deco pieces and comprise rust, cobalt, leaf green and ochre.

'Chimneys' (picture page 79)

Date of manufacture 1930s
Backstamp: 5

Solid slabs of colour are applied to the pottery using a sponged technique, and these consist of cobalt, rust, ochre and green. Black lines and white rectangles are used to break up the colours and a chimney pot arrangement appears to be belching small spouts of black smoke.

Delhi (picture page 79)

Date of manufacture 1930+
Pattern number 9833
Backstamp 47

A hand painted design in intensely vivid colours. The setting sun throws out wide yellow and orange-red rays against a cobalt blue sky. A curved tree has arching foliage, shaped like green clouds which spans the scene. Pale purple hills are in the background with green fields to the fore, together with bright over-lapping discs of colour.

A page from a contemporary catalogue describes the pattern as being in 'Jazz colourings of brilliant reds, blues and greens. Hand painted'.

'Flames' (picture page 80)

Date of manufacture 1930+
Pattern number 4015
Backstamp 4, 22, 48

This pattern was designed by Ike Mattison and some pieces of ware carry his personal backstamp. Unfortunately, once again a blank has been drawn regarding history, and it has not been possible to find out anything about the artist.

'Flames' is a striking design, principally in colours of yellow, orange-red and black. Flames appear to emanate from a large round black spot, going both upwards and downwards. Irregular outlines are filled with the same colours and green, blue and light purple are additionally used. On some items, half a stylised flowerhead can be seen.

The range was issued primarily as table ware with tea pots, coffee pots, jugs and cups and saucers being found.

'Geometric Tulips' (picture page 80)

Date of manufacture 1930s
Pattern number 1194
Backstamp 49

This design is hand painted and has a mottled or sponged finish. Colours of cobalt, ochre, green, orange, mauve, light blue and black are spread across the piece in blocks and other angular, random shapes, outlined in black. Three orange tulips give the pattern its name and these are arranged in a 'stepped' manner against mauve and black.

'Jazz' (picture page 80)

Date of manufacture 1930+
Backstamp 9

Difficult to describe, the 'Jazz' pattern uses arcs and fans, circles, squares and triangles to great effect, combining the various shapes with colours of rich yellow, orange red, rust, green, purple, black and white. It gained its name, given to it by collectors, from the black and white squares arranged rather like musical notations.

Jazz has only ever been seen used on coffee ware and it is rumoured that it was sold through the pages of a women's magazine as a special offer. There is no pattern number, but the coffee pot bears the patent number 301262.

'Jigsaw' (picture page 81)

Date of manufacture 1930s
Backstamp 4

The interlocking pattern is transfer printed on to a beige-tan ground, with additional colour being hand painted. Orange, purple and yellow have been used, although the yellow is almost indistinguishable against the ground colour. A splash of green is found on the handle of the jug.

Persian

Date of manufacture 1930+
Pattern number 9882

Two fruit bowls poorly illustrated by *The Pottery Gazette* in November 1930 appear to be mainly of solid colour with broad, irregular geometric designs at the rim. A jam pot, also featured, shows slashes of geometric shapes. No colours are mentioned in the accompanying text.

'Polka Dot' (picture page 81)

Date of manufacture 1950s
Backstamp 13

A simple polka dot design which is strikingly effective. The colours are reversed on the bedside set, giving relief from the bright scarlet used on the tray.

'Red Roof House' – Atlas China (picture page 81)

Date of manufacture 1930s
Pattern number 7363
Backstamp 21

Totally different from the Red Roof pattern in the Hand Painted chapter, the house is depicted in typical Art Deco fashion. The colours are bright and typical of the period. The roof of the house is in orange, and a curving plume of lilac smoke issues from the chimney. Lilac is also used to suggest the shadows. The stylised trees are in yellow, green and cobalt, and yellow, cobalt and lilac. Flowers are portrayed rather like lollipops on sticks and are painted orange and cobalt. The scene stands out vividly against the fine white china background.

'Tulips' (picture page 81)

Date of manufacture 1930+
Pattern number 9977
Backstamp 50

Hand painted stylised tulips in colours of orange, purple and yellow are set randomly against a background of criss-crossing leaves in light and dark green. Patches of cobalt blue, purple and grey form the background. Although stylised, the design is less angular than 'Geometric Tulips' (above).

'Wheels'

(picture page 82)

Date of manufacture 1930s
Pattern number 9900
Backstamp 50

A wheel-like arrangement of colours form the basis for this pattern. The 'spokes' of the wheels are in cobalt and orange, while the white ground is broken up by broad brush strokes in green and black with occasional splashes of citrus yellow.

Anne Hathaway's Cottage: Biscuit barrel, teapot, condiment set with Art Deco carrying handle.

Anne Hathaway's Cottage: Dessert plate, tea plate, table lamp, sugar shaker, cruet, sugar shaker (a later version, less well-modelled).

GRIMWADES LTD. :: STOKE-ON-TRENT
(Incorporating Rubian Art Pottery & Atlas China)

"Olde England"
Table Ware
(Hand-painted).

A distinct novelty for table use. The modelling is in high relief and all the color work done by hand.

The illustration faithfully represents the subject. An old world cottage complete with thatched and lichened roof, timbered walls and garden.

Item No.					Price per dozen
1.	Covered Butter	...	...	...	24/-
2.	Cruet—3 pieces on Tray		...	...	24/-
3.	Cheese	...	...	...	30/-
4.	Teapot S/S., 18ozs. capacity	...		...	30/-
5.	Covered Biscuit Jar with Wicker handle		...	39/-
6.	Marmalade and Stand		...	...	21/-

Item No.				Price per dozen
7.	Uncovered Jug, 18 ozs. capacity		...	21/-
8.	Condiment Set (Salt & Pepper on Tray)	...	18/-
9.	Covered Jug, 17 ozs. capacity	...	...	28/-
10.	Sugar, 3" diameter	...	...)	30/- per doz. pairs
12.	Cream, 9 ozs. capacity	...)		
11.	Teapot L/S, 27 ozs. capacity	...	36/- per dozen	
	also Teapot Stand for L/S Pot	...	9/- per dozen	

Can also supply :—

Sugar Sifter ... ... **14/-** per dozen

Cigarette Box, covered ... **24/-** per dozen

Sherwin & Co. (Hanley), Ltd., Printers.

Olde England: Advertising sheet issued by Grimwades. (Courtesy Peter Greenhalf)

Olde England: Cheese dish, condiment set, biscuit barrel.

Olde England: Dessert plates in 2 colourways.

Shakespeare's Birthplace: Dessert plate.

Ye Olde Inne (red roof): 4-piece tea service given as a premium with coupons collected by the customer.

Ye Olde Inne: Biscuit barrel (red roof), dessert plate, cheese dish, preserve pot, sugar shaker and condiment set (all grey roof).

Ye Olde Mill (red roof): Cheese dish, milk jug, teapot.

Ye Olde Mill (pink roof): Dessert plate, hot water jug, teapot, sugar shaker, salt and pepper pots, cup and saucer (rare), cheese dish.

Top left: Apple preserve pot. Below right: Wishing Well preserve pot.

Beehive: Biscuit barrel in a seldom-seen pale turquoise blue.

Beehive: Teapot, cream and sugar set in the tan colourway.

Beehive: Biscuit barrel, dessert plate, covered butter, condiment set, all in the tan colourway.

Beehive (shown in various colourways): Small oval bowl, sugar shaker (tan/lilac), sugar shaker (cream), preserve pot (tan), cheese dish (cream), toast rack (primrose), preserve pot with fast stand (tan).

Castle on the Hill: Cheese dish.

Chanticleer: Cheese dish in the cream colourway.

Chanticleer: Three teapots in differing colourways.

Chanticleer (shown in various colourways): preserve pot, milk jug, sugar shaker, preserve pot (all in brown), cruet set (blue), sugar bowl (cream), condiment set (brown), sugar shaker (cream).

Countryside: Sweetmeat dish.

Crocus: Sundae dish, sugar shaker, Lotus: Preserve pot.

Dovecote: Shallow fruit bowl with a matt glaze; vase TAME shape, showing the pattern on the reverse. .

Galleon: Biscuit box with silver plated cover.

Game (dark blue colourway): Sugar shaker, biscuit barrel.

Game (cream colourway): Vase in the TIBER shape.

GRIMWADES LTD. :: STOKE-ON-TRENT

(Incorporating Rubian Art Pottery & Atlas China)

Royal Winton
"Gera"
No. 2209.

A most attractive adaptation in strong relief of the popular Geranium Foliage and Flower in natural colours with an appropriate Rustic background.

This design is made in three distinct colourings other than the illustration. It is impossible to describe them, but small sample pieces can be supplied.

PRICE LIST.

Item No.		Price
1. Cheese		21/- per doz.
2. Toast-Rack, 3 bar		12/- „ „
Also 5 bar		15/- „ „
3. Sugar, 4" diameter	} 16/- per doz. pairs.
4. Cream, 6½ ozs. capacity	
5. Covered Butter		21/- per doz.
6. Mint Boat and Stand		12/- „ „
7. Marmalade and Stand		20/- „ „
8. Cup and Saucer, tea size		12/- „ „
Also Tea Plate (See Illustration No. 14)		6/- „ „
9. Cake Comport, 8½" diameter, 2" high		30/- „ „
10. 3 Compartment Tray		33/- „ „
11. Twin Tray		18/- „ „
12. Sweet, 6" diameter		8/- „ „
„ 7" „		10/- „ „
„ 8" „		12/- „ „
Shallow Fruit (same shape as illustration No. 12, but 9½" diameter)		24/- „ „
13. Dessert Plate, 8" diameter		14/- „ „
14. Tea or Sandwich Plate, 6½" diameter		6/- „ „

Item No.		Price
15. Covered Jug, 23 ozs. capacity		24/- per doz.
16. Teapot, 33 ozs. capacity		33/- „ „
Also Teapot Stand		8/6 „ „
17. Condiment Set (Salt and Pepper on Tray) ...		12/- „ „
18. Salad Bowl, 9½" diameter		33/- „ „
And Salad Servers		15/- doz. pairs
19. Cruet Set, 3 pieces on Tray		18/- per doz.
20. Sandwich Tray, 12½" × 7"		30/- „ „
Sandwich Set, 7 pieces		5/6 per set
Comprising :—1 Tray as No. 20 6 Plates as No. 14		
21. Sugar Sifter		12/- per doz.
22. Cake Plate, handled		18/- „ „
Also made :—		
Jug, 30's, 42 ozs. capacity		20/- „ „
„ 36's, 34 „ „		18/- „ „
„ 42's, 26 „ „		16/- „ „
„ 48's, 19 „ „		14/- „ „
„ 54's, 14 „ „		12/- „ „
Shape as Illustration No. 15, but without cover.		

H

Sherwin & Co. (Hanley). Ltd., Printers.

Gera: Contemporary advertising sheet issued by Grimwades. (Courtesy Peter Greenhalf)

Gera (in various colourways): Dessert plate, teaplate (both black), shallow dessert bowl (cream), hot water jug and stand (blue), sugar shaker (green), sugar shaker, mint boat and stand (cream).

Grapes: Preserve pot with fast stand.

Haystack: Teapot.

Lakeland: Two flower holders and a candlestick.

Iris: Tall flower vase (14½ inches high).

Lakeland (yellow colourway): Dessert plate and preserve pot.

Lakeland: Teapot, hot water jug, milk jug, tea plate, sugar bowl.

Lakeland: Dessert plate, sugar shaker, twin tray, salt and mustard pots, mint boat and stand.

Pagoda: Sugar shaker, twin tray, condiment set, 3-bar toast rack.

Peony: Muffin dish, 3-bar toast rack, preserve pot.

Pixie (pastel colourway): Wall clock, milk jug, sugar shaker (black pixie), preserve pot with fast stand (showing only the fruit detail), preserve pot, 3-bar toast rack, sugar shaker.

Pixie (dark green pixie): Cheese dish, sugar shaker, hot water jug, teapot, mint boat and stand.

Pixie (dark red pixie): Dessert plate, sugar shaker, large jug, condiment set, mint boat, cream jug.

GRIMWADES LTD. :: STOKE-ON-TRENT
(Incorporating Rubian Art Pottery & Atlas China)

"Primula"
Table Ware
(Hand-painted)

The treatment of this popular subject (as illustrated) provides a contrast to the purely natural, as the foliage background is in rich old ivory with delicate hand-tracing in brown, thus emphasising the rich coloring of the flowers in a very striking manner.

Made in three varieties :—

No. 1847. Cardinal Red Flowers as illustrated.

No. 1848. Sweet Pink Flowers.

No. 1802. Delicate Blue Flowers.

Item No.		Price
1.	Sandwich Tray, 12½" x 7½"	30 - per doz.
2.	Sandwich Plate, 6" diameter	6 -
	Sandwich Set 7 pieces	
	1 Tray as No. 1	5 6 per set
	6 Plates as No. 2	
3.	Salad Bowl, 9½" diameter	42 - per doz.
4.	Cake Comport, 9" diameter, 3½" high	33 -
	Dessert Set 7 pieces	
	1 Comport as No. 4	9 9 per set
	6 Dessert Plates as No. 6	
5.	Teapot S/S, 23 ozs. capacity	27 - per doz.
	L/S, 33 ozs.	33 -
	Also Teapot Stand	10 -
6.	Dessert Plate, 8" diameter	14 -
		Per dozen
7.	Jug S/S, 23 ozs. capacity	15 - or
	M/S, 30 ozs.	18 - 4 6
	L/S, 40 ozs.	21 - set 3 pcs.
		Can also supply :—
	Eggset, 4 Cups	21 - per doz.
	Triple Tray	36 -
	Mint Boat and Stand	12 -
	Sugar, 3½" Diam., and Cream, 5½ ozs. capacity,	
	Bridge size	16 - per dozen pairs
	Milk Jug, uncovered, 1 pint (Shape as No. 11),	
	actual capacity 24 ozs.	18 - per doz.
	Fruit Dish, 8½" diameter	24 -
	Flower Holder L/S, 6½" high	54 -
	S/S, 5½" high	36 -
	Candy-Jar, covered	36 -
	Watercress and Stand, 8½" diameter	43 -
	Covered Powder Box	21 -

Item No.		Price
8.	Twin Tray	24 - per doz.
9.	Cheese S/S	21 -
	L/S	30 -
10.	Marmalade and Stand	21 -
11.	Covered Jug, 24 ozs. capacity	24 -
12.	Cruet, 3 pieces on Tray	21 -
	Also Condiment Set (Salt & Pepper on Tray)	15 -
14.	Sugar Sifter	18 -
15.	Toast-Rack, 5 bar	16 -
	Also 3 bar	12 6
16.	Sweet, 5"	8 -
	6"	10 6
	7"	12 6
	8"	15 -

ATLAS CHINA

Item No.		Price
13.	Cup and Saucer, Tea size	17 - per doz.
	Also supplied :—	
	Tea Plates	13 - per doz.
	Afternoon Sugars and Creams	20 - per dozen pairs
	Teaset 21 pieces	21 - per set
	Teaset 40 pieces	38 6 per set

Sherwin & Co. (Hanley), Ltd., Printers.

Primula: Advertising leaflet issued by Grimwades. (Courtesy Peter Greenhalf)

65

Primula (various colourways): Oval dessert dish, teapot stand, preserve pot, mint boat.

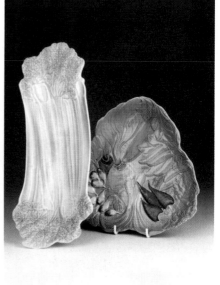

Regina (various colourways): Biscuit barrel, square dessert dish, 3 cruets, hot water jug.

Salad: Rhubarb dish, triangular serving dish.

Terrace: Vase in the Moreton shape, 2 other vases, charger (diameter 11½ inches).

Terrace (in two colourways): 2 dessert plates, sugar bowl for cubed sugar, with silver plated lid and integral tongs), condiment set.

Trellis Rose Garden: Dessert plate, cream jug, sugar shaker, teapot, 3-bar toast rack, condiment set.

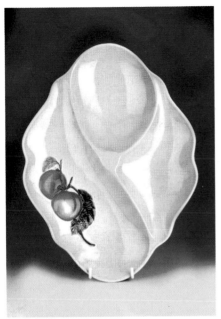

Apple: Hors d'oeuvre dish.

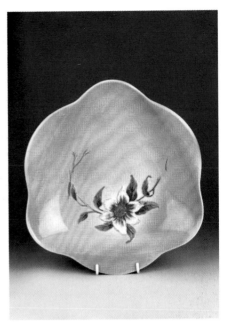

Apple Blossom: Shallow serving dish.

Briar: Diamond shaped dish, sugar shaker (cream), toast rack, sugar shaker (green).

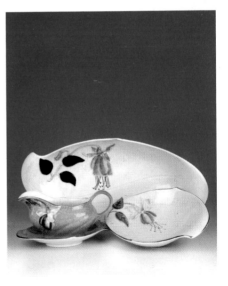

Fuchsia: Oval dish, mint boat and stand (mottled), sweetmeat dish.

Honey Lily: Oval dish, smaller oval dish in cream with striped border, cup and saucer, mint boat, 5-bar toast rack, pair of salad servers.

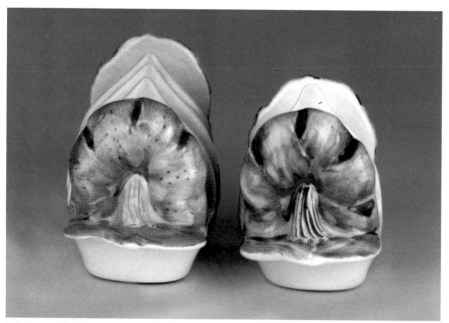

Left: Honey Lily 5-bar toast rack; Right: Hibiscus 3-bar toast rack. Note the differences in the hand painting on the petals.

Pansy: Large hors d'oeuvre dish, tiny pin tray.   *Petunia (yellow): 5-bar toast rack.*

Petunia (pink): Shaped dessert dish, milk jug, large milk jug, cruet set, tennis cup and saucer.

Rosebud (yellow): Coffee pot, chocolate comport, preserve pot, teapot, cup and saucer.

Rosebud (pink): Bread and butter plate, cup (cream), butter dish, preserve pot.

Rosebud (green): Coffee pot, 5-bar toast rack, condiment set, preserve pot, tennis cup and saucer.

Rosebud (green): Bread and butter plate, cheese dish, milk jug, candlestick, trinket pot, cruet.

Rosebud (green): Salad bowl and servers.

Tea Rose (various colours): Oval serving plate, wall pocket, dessert dish, candy box.

Thistle: Preserve pot, candlestick.

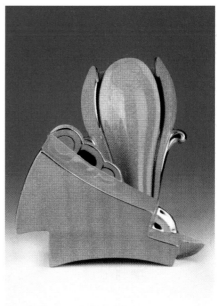

Plain Colours: Wall clock in shaded green and blue.

Mottled Ware: Wall pocket in the NITA shape, Art Deco wall pocket in the ROSA shape.

Delphinium: Large dished plaque (diameter 12¹/₂ inches). Signed W.H.

Galleon: Table lamp base. Poplars: Jug in the REMUS shape (height 7³/₄ inches).

Red Roof: Plate in the ASCOT shape (9 inches diameter)

Red Roof: Close up, showing the pattern in detail.

'6742': Large hand painted dished plaque (diameter 12½ inches) signed F. Phillips, transfer printed bread and butter plate.

Anemone: Coffee set.

Anemone: Small oval dish (diameter 5¹/₂ inches).
Fruit: Basket in the KEW shape (height 6¹/₂ inches).

Fruit: Ornamental jug.

Game Birds: Tobacco jar.

Roses: Table lamp base.

78

Blocks: Cup in the Art Deco style.

Chimneys: Bedside set with integral toast rack, comprising cup, cream and sugar set.

Dehli: Shaped oblong serving plate (length 11½ inches), teapot in the COUNTESS shape.

Flames: Jug in the CAMBRIDGE shape, oval sweetmeat dish, tea plate, COUNTESS shaped hot water jug

Geometric Tulips: Jug in the GLOBE shape, large tea plate

Jazz: Part coffee set in the WINTON shape.

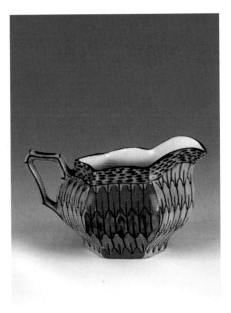

Jigsaw: Cream jug in the HECTOR shape.

Polka Dot: Bedside set comprising teapot, cup, cream and sugar set and toast rack.

Red Roof House – Atlas China: coffee cup and saucer.

Tulips: Chocolate comport in the GREEK shape.

Wheels: Small unlidded pot.

Apples: Chamber pot. (Courtesy Peter Greenhalf)

Asters: Cream fruit bowl (diameter 8 inches), green jug (height 8 inches).

Autumn Leaves: Charger in green colourway (diameter 13 inches), covered vase in the CHINESE JAR shape in dark red colourway (height 11½ inches overall).

Aztec Fringe: Covered vase (height 9 inches overall).

Bubbles (orange): Art Deco shaped fruit bowl (diameter 9 inches).

Bubbles (green): Shaped fruit bowl (diameter 9½ inches).

Butterfly: Small, shaped trinket box (diagonal width 4 inches).

Castle by the Lake: Bowl (diameter 10 ½ inches).

Cherries: vase in the VIENNA shape (height 6¾ inches

Cherry Blossom (various colourways): Floating (flower) bowl in the BUTE shape (diameter 10½ inches), soap dish, sugar shaker.

Carnation: Left: Vase in the CINTRA shape (height 8 inches), Right: vase in the ROMA shape (height 8¹/₄ inches) Front row: covered biscuit box, GLOBE jug

Chinese Dragon: Jug in the REMUS shape (height 8½ inches), bud vase (height 4½ inches).

Chrysanthemum: Jug in the RONDA shape (height 8½ inches).

Courtship: Small dish in the BUTE floating bowl style (diameter 5¾ inches).

Crazy Paving: Jug in the REMUS shape (height 8½ inches), vase in the BOUQUET shape (height 6¼ inches).

Daisies: Art Deco shaped wall pocket.

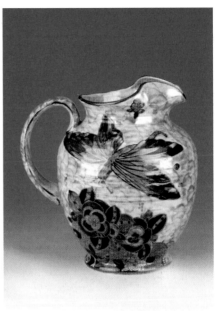

Dragonfly: Jug (height 8¹/₄ inches).

Fairy Cobwebs: Plate in the ASCOT shape (diameter 9 inches), flower vase (height 9 inches).

Fruit: Part sandwich set in the OCTAGON shape.

Floral Bouquet: Biscuit barrel with silver plated lid.

Fuchsia: Vase in the CAPRI shape (height 7 inches).

Galleon: Plate in the OCTAGON shape (diameter 9 inches), vase in the VIENNA shape (height 6³/₄ inches).

Garland: Covered vase in the GORDON shape (height 8 inches overall).

Hollyhocks: Vase (height 7 inches).

Honeysuckle: Jardinière in the ARGYLE shape.

89

Humming Birds: Chamber pot.

Ming: Floating bowl in the GREEK shape (diameter 10½ inches) together with a GOLDEN ORIOLE bird flower holder and ARBOR Floweraid.

Hydrangea: Basket in the ESSEX shape (length 11 inches), wall pocket in the NITA shape.

Lakeside Flowers: Octagonal vase (height 7³/₄ inches), columnar vase (height 8 inches), shaped oval dish (length 12 inches).

Leaves: Tobacco jar.

Nasturtium: Jug in the RONDA shape (height 8¹/₂ inches).

Page from a Grimwades catalogue showing floating bowls and table centres in BUTE, CECIL and OCTAGON shapes, together with ARBOR Floweraid and perching rim bird.

Peacock: Plate (diameter 10 inches).

Petunias: Ribbed jug (height 9 inches).

Pheasant: Biscuit plate in the octagon shape (diameter 5 inches).

Plums: Teapot in the SEXTA shape.

Poppies: Nut dish with cut-out handles (diameter 5¾ inches). This would originally have had a small scoop with it.

Romance: Footed cake comport (diameter 9½ inches).

Scrolls and Flowers: Bowl (13 inches diameter).

Shells: Candy Box.

Silver Birch: Plate (diameter 12 inches).

Standard Rose Bush: Ribbed jug (height 9 inches).

Stylised Flowers: Ashtray (width 8½ inches).

Summer Bouquet: Pot pourri vase and cover (height 6½ inches overall).

95

Sunburst: Vase in the REMUS shape (height 8¹/₂ inches).

Trees and Roses: Jug in the RONDA shape (height 8¹/₂ inches).

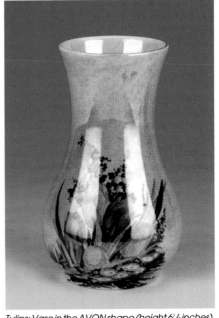

Tudor Rose: Tea plate.

Tulips: Vase in the AVON shape (height 6¹/₂ inches).

Trailing Harebells: Plate (diameter 10½ inches).

Watteau: Shaving mug.

Winter Flowers: Tea plate.

Yellow Iris: Flower vase (height 7 inches, width 10 inches).

Plain Colours: Advertising ashtray made for Comoy's of London; shaped bowl introduced in a Grimwades catalogue for 1925-28 as a basket in the NORMA shape (width 8 inches).

Plain Colours: Tobacco jar, advertising ashtray made for the 'Reedhill Finishing Co. Ltd.'.

Golden Age: Cornucopia shaped vase (height 7 inches), cream and sugar set.

Musical Jug made for the coronation of George VI showing front (right) and reverse (left). Courtesy of Royal Winton International Collectors Club)

Left to right: Annie Laurie, Come to the Fair, Floral Dance.

Left to right: Killarney, Phil the Fluters Ball, Sarie Marais.

Left to right: Stirling Castle, There is a Tavern in the Town, Under the Spreading Chestnut Tree.

General Douglas MacArthur (3 sizes).

Left to right: Uncle Sam (small and medium size), John Bull (medium size).

General Sir Archibald Wavell (large size).

Mr Pickwick, stoppered container.

Indian Chief (large and medium size).

Mr Bumble and Sairey Gamp (height 7¹/₂ inches).

Mr Bumble: Pair of bookends (height 8¹/₄ inches).

Left to right: A Token of Love (height 9^1/$_2$ inches), Masquerade (height 8^1/$_2$ inches), Romance (height 9^1/$_2$ inches).

Lustre Ware

Although lustre ware was not entirely new to Grimwades, (the Jacobean pattern issued around 1913 had a lustred finish), it really took off with the introduction of a new range marketed under the name of Byzanta Ware in 1925. A special Byzanta Ware backstamp was introduced, although this can sometimes be extremely difficult to see, especially when transfer printed on a dark ground.

The new ware was advertised extensively by the company as early as May 1925, and it was intended to capture a large section of the Christmas trade for that year. The range consisted, primarily, of 'fancies', although practical items such as toilet sets were manufactured. *The Pottery Gazette* gave it a favourable write-up, describing it as 'a very smart range'.

Initially, the company concentrated on flower bowls, jardinières and table centres. The flower bowls were large, round and shallow, and were available in two sizes – 9 inches and 10 inches – and cost respectively, 12/6d (62¹/₂p) and 13/6d (67¹/₂p).

In addition, customers were able to buy round Floweraids (Registered number 690980) in solid black to place in the centre of the bowl. These blocks held the blooms in place in order to make a pleasing flower arrangement. Alternatively, a lustred 'tree trunk', known as the 'Arobor' Floweraid, could be bought for a cost of 1/- (5p) extra, into which blossoms were then inserted and these were also available in plain black. A further alternative consisted of a hand painted bird, perched on a similar tree trunk, and used for the same flower arranging purpose (see Ming entry). Rim birds were also available for 1/9d (9p) each and these perched on the rim of the bowl.

The table centre, with the bowl set on a pedestal stand, was also available in two sizes – 8 inches and 10 inches – and cost a little more at 11/6d (57¹/₂p) and 15/6d (77¹/₂p) respectively. The Floweraids could also be used with these.

The Pottery Gazette was enthusiastic about the new lustre ware and waxed lyrical in October 1925. 'Patterns which call for a special mention are the No. 4274 – a treatment of tulips in a dark lustred blue – and the No. 7606 – a decoration having for its inspiration a bunch of cherries, executed in the "Byzanta" lustre style. The "Greek" shape rosebowl is seen to advantage in a Gobelin blue. No fewer than fifty varieties are available in the new table centres, which have for their object the economising of table space.'

The new range proved so popular that Grimwades extended it to include table ware, concentrating especially on sandwich sets, known also as supper sets. Vases and ornamental jugs were also included, as were baskets, biscuit boxes, fruit bowls, trinket boxes and even shaving mugs. Most of the designs were highlighted by the addition of gilding, done by hand, with the company using 'the best burnished gold'.

Plain colours were used without ornamentation and these were generally teamed together, such as Gobelin blue and yellow, or Gobelin blue combined with a vivid orange, which Grimwades called Tangerine. Items of a dark red colour, using no other decoration other than rim gilding, formed a range known as Rubay Ware.

When used with other designs, the ground colours were either pale and in shades of blue, yellow, green, pink and cream, or were vivid in dark blue, orange, or rich ruby red known by the company as Marone. Occasionally, designs were further enhanced with dots and splashes of enamel colours which were applied by hand. The majority of patterns and designs were based on plants and flowers, although there were some Art Deco influences.

In 1937, *The Pottery Gazette* announced that 'a new series of ornamental wares has been produced, inspired by the old and thoroughly successful "Byzanta" ware. The colours, which are underglaze, are rich and intensive, such as ruby and mazarine blue, and the patternings are strongly traced in gold by hand.'

Lustre ware remained in production throughout the years, although colours in the 1950s are weaker, the designs less well portrayed and less imaginative.

In the late 1950s, the company marketed a range of gold and silver lustre ware intended for wedding anniversaries. Tea ware was produced as well as a selection of vases. The gold range was left plain, but the silver sometimes had a hammered finish.

It is impossible to know exactly how many lustre patterns were produced over the years. New patterns are frequently discovered and, doubtless, more will come to light after the publication of this book.

'Apples' (picture page 82)

Date of manufacture 1925+
Backstamp 51

Several apples can be seen hanging from a gnarled branch. The fruit is depicted in glowing autumn tones accentuated by green leaves. The ground colour is Gobelin blue and the interior is finished in a mother-of-pearl lustre.

'Asters' (picture page 82)

Date of manufacture 1930s
Pattern number 5284 (cream ground); 5285 (green ground)
Backstamp 7

Although the leaves in this pattern look more like those of the chrysanthemum, the flower closely resembles that of an aster. Two large blooms dominate the foreground, with leafy buds shown above. Other unidentifiable flowers are massed alongside.

In the cream colourway, the flowers are in shades of yellow and beige with the foliage picked out in dark brown, light green and dark green. In the green colourway, the flowers are delicately painted in pink and blue and the foliage is both light and dark green.

'Autumn Leaves' (picture page 83)

Date of manufacture 1930s
Pattern number 4194 (red ground) 4233 (green ground)
Backstamp 6

The ground colours of dark red, almost maroon, and the alternative colourway of a pale khaki green, set off the autumnal colours of this pattern. Leaves and blossoms are portrayed in a stylised manner and are in muted shades of green, yellow, ochre, tan, blue and pink.

'Aztec Fringe' (picture page 83)

Date of manufacture 1925+
Backstamp 51

This pattern shows Art Deco influences. Multi-coloured pennants decorate the rim of the vase in a fringed manner (see illustration). Above are solid circles of colour, together with a geometric border in blocks of pink and dark blue. The ground colour is mid-blue, the interior being a vivid orange. This orange is also used on the main pattern together with yellow and green. The lid is decorated with a band of daisy-like flowers in white and yellow, separated from each other by gilding.

The plate illustrated shows the flowers in profile, set in a band around a circular motif.

'Bubbles' (picture page 83)

Date of manufacture 1930s
Pattern number 4071 (orange ground); 5280 (green ground)
Backstamp 6, 7

When executed in the vivid orange typical of Byzanta ware, this is one of the more dramatic lustre patterns. Stylised flower heads are in shades of yellow, deep turquoise, green, blue, dark pink, tan, lilac and purple, and these are surrounded by a myriad of bubbles in green, tan and lilac.

The green colourway is less dramatic, the decoration being kept to a minimum. The flower heads are in yellow, tan, dark pink and maroon, with the bubbles merely being outlined in dark brown.

It has also been seen on a pink ground.

'Butterfly' (picture page 84)

Date of manufacture 1925+
Backstamp 51

The only example of this pattern so far found is the trinket box illustrated. The base is coloured a rich orange, with the interior having a mother-of-pearl finish. The butterfly is painted in naturalistic colours of rust and black against a pale yellow ground.

Carnation (picture page 85)

Date of manufacture 1930s

Pattern number 2322
Backstamp 6, 52

This is perhaps the most widely known and most collected of all the lustre patterns, and one which is actually named by Grimwades. The ground colour is sponged in shades of cream and tan and is an excellent foil for the multi-coloured carnations. These are portrayed in yellow, combined with pink and purple, and in apple green and yellow, combined with sage green and pale purple. The stylised leaves are in tan, cobalt, lilac and dark green. There are also additional dots of bright turquoise enamelling. The pattern is further enhanced by gilded fronds. Where there is an interior colour, this is sponged in pale blue and lilac.

'Castle by the Lake' (picture page 84)

Date of manufacture 1930s
Pattern number 4581
Backstamp 6

A more unusual scenic design is set against orange lustre. A turreted castle is in the background portrayed by a simple line drawing. The foreground consists of a lake in purples and mauve with stylised water lilies in white and yellow with dark pink stamens. Irises also occupy the foreground and these are in white, blue and orange, the leaves in a vivid green. In the middle ground, black trees are silhouetted against the orange sky. The colour on the reverse of the bowl is also orange.

'Cherries' (picture page 84)

Date of manufacture 1925+
Backstamp 51

Four cherries hang gracefully from the branch of a tree and are painted in tones of red and yellow. The leaves are green and, out of sight, small buds of blossom can be found in white and yellow. The ground colour is a mottled mid-blue.

'Cherry Blossom' (picture page 84)

Date of manufacture 1925+
Pattern number 4820 (blue ground)
Backstamp 51

Used as a rim decoration, branches of cherry blossom are arranged against a curved, stylised border painted in dark blue. In the blue colourway, the branches are green, the flowers pink and white. Interior sponging is in deep pink. In the orange colourway, the flowers are yellow with pink centres and are set against green branches.

'Chinese Dragon' (picture page 86)

Date of manufacture 1930s
Pattern number Possibly 2271
Backstamp 6

An exotic pattern that flows across the deep red ground which is given texture by small irregular outlines in a darker colour. The dragon undulates in an oriental fashion and is portrayed in turquoise, green, tan, purple and yellow. The scales are hand enamelled in pale turquoise, the tail and legs are dotted with enamel of the same colour, while the head and body have splashes of enamel in vivid orange. A scrolled border in cobalt and gilt is at the base, while at the rim are abstract shapes in cobalt, tan, green and lilac.

'Chrysanthemum' (picture page 86)

Date of manufacture 1930s
Pattern number 2134
Backstamp 6

Curly-petalled blooms of the chrysanthemum form the basis for this design. The flowers are cream, with the petals highlighted by white enamelling, while the centres are picked out in orange enamel. The leaves are bronze and black and tend to disappear against the vivid cobalt ground. Near the top of the piece can be seen a gilt spider's web which stands out against the pale blue. Yellow sponging has been used for the interior colour.

'Courtship' (picture page 86)

Date of manufacture 1925+
Backstamp 51

Stylised blue trees are seen moulded in relief against a cobalt sky. A woman wearing a green dress is seen seated by a river in the foreground. Her companion leans on her chair, his dog at his feet. He wears a yellow cap, a pink doublet, lavender breeches and yellow hose.

'Crazy Paving' (picture page 86)

Date of manufacture 1930s
Pattern numbers 2997 (pink ground), possibly 2258 (cream ground)
Backstamp 7

Random bands and blocks resembling crazy paving in a rich brown give this pattern its name. The stylised flowers resemble those used in the 'Bubbles' pattern (above) and, in the cream mottled colourway, are painted in colours of dark pink, purple, cobalt, tan, pale pink, yellow, green and purple. The leaves are both light and dark green.

The pink colourway is rather more vivid with the flowers in deep pink, purple, lilac, ochre, pale blue and pale green. The leaves are a deep turquoise, cobalt, purple and brown. The pink ground has been painted to have a scale effect.

'Daisies' (picture page 87)

Date of manufacture 1930s
Backstamp 7

Stylised daisies and other flowers are seen set beside a boulder. The flowers are in shades of pink, yellow, green and deep turquoise. The ground colour is sponged orange.

'Dragonfly' (picture page 87)

Date of manufacture 1930s
Backstamp 6

A large dragonfly hovers above grouped stylised flowers and leaves and seems to shimmer against a pink scale ground. The body of the insect is yellow, the wings are green shading to yellow, with the tips a dark red shading to purple and blue. The flowers are in strong colours of dark red, ochre, blue, cobalt and purple with the leaves being dark and light green and banded with yellow and brown. Scrolling ornamentation at the base of the pattern is in tan and grey.

'Fairy Cobwebs' (picture page 87)

Date of manufacture 1930s
Pattern number 2351
Backstamp 6

A very pretty pattern, portraying the yellow-haired figure of a fairy perched on the branch of a cherry tree. She is dressed in shades of pink and lilac with wings in yellow, pink and green. Two green butterflies hover near her feet and to her left is suspended a gilt cobweb. The cherry blossom is in warm tones of pink and apricot which contrasts delicately with the dark blue ground.

Floating Bowls and Table Centres (picture page 92)

Date of manufacture 1925+

Floating bowls were large, round, shallow flower bowls with incurving rims – a shape known as Bute. They were intended for use with an 'Arbor' Floweraid. It is presumed that flowerheads were floated on to the water in the bowl, with sprigs or sprays of blossom being inserted into the Floweraid. Some floating bowls had straight sides and these were made in the Greek shape.

The table centres, which could be used for flowers or fruit, were floating Bute-shaped bowls set on pedestals; an alternative was the Cecil shape which curved in rather more, and which had tiny club-shaped cut-outs near the rim. The Octagon was a plain 8-sided bowl set on a pedestal.

Rim birds, set on springs, could be attached to the side of the bowls (see also Ming).

'Floral Bouquet'

Date of manufacture 1930s
Pattern number 298
Backstamp 7

The orange ground helps lift the rather muted colours of the flowers and leaves in this pattern. Shades of dark pink, yellow, turquoise and light green are used, with additional emphasis being given by the black in-fill and shadowing between the flowers and leaves.

'Fruit'

(picture page 88)

Date of manufacture 1930s
Pattern number 7899
Backstamp 3

The fruit is in this pattern is extremely well-portrayed and enhanced with gilded outlines. The central grouping consists of a pear, an apple, a peach together with strawberries, gooseberries and redcurrants. The border comprises grapes, raspberries, plums and cherries – and all are painted in naturalistic colours. The blue ground darkens into cobalt at the rim. The ground colour on the reverse is a rich burgundy.

'Fuchsia'

(picture page 88)

Date of manufacture 1930s
Pattern number 4418
Backstamp 9

Strong mottled orange has been used for the ground colour with mid-blue being used for the interior. The flowers, painted in shades of cobalt and lavender, are seen suspended from a yellow branch. The decoration is minimal, but striking in its simplicity.

'Galleon'

(picture page 89)

Date of manufacture 1930s
Pattern number 4953
Backstamp 1

Billowing sails send this sailing ship scudding across the stormy sea, making for a dramatic design. The ground colour is dark blue and the sails are portrayed in various shades of yellow and tan, the hull being picked out in yellow, blue and dark pink. The sea is blue, green and black, with the horizon shown as a thin yellow line; threatening clouds are traced in gilt. The border pattern depicts Viking ships in yellow and dark pink. The reverse and interior ground colours are vivid orange.

'Garland'   (picture page 89)

Date of manufacture 1930s
Pattern number possibly 4456
Backstamp 3

Unidentifiable flowers and leaves are shown in deep pink, lavender pink and two shades of green, and are arranged in a wreath or garland against a cobalt blue mottled ground.

'Hollyhocks'   (picture page 89)

Date of manufacture 1950s+
Backstamp 19

A later example of Grimwades lustre ware, and not really comparable with earlier pieces – the colours are pale and the design less well-drawn. Sprays of hollyhocks in pink and blue are set against an iridescent, mother-of-pearl ground.

'Honeysuckle'   (picture page 89)

Date of manufacture 1925+
Backstamp 51

The decoration on the jardinière illustrated is minimal, consisting of honeysuckle flowers and leaves set on a wide band of cobalt blue. The flowers are depicted in cream and a pale apricot, with leaves in green and petrol blue. A narrow band of turquoise underlined in green adds definition above and below the pattern. The ground colour is mottled blue and the interior is bright orange.

'Humming Birds'   (picture page 90)

Date of manufacture 1925+
Backstamp 51

Dark blue trees are silhouetted against the Gobelin blue ground to great effect, while humming birds in green, yellow and blue dart among the branches. The interior has a mother-of-pearl finish.

'Hydrangea'   (picture page 90)

Date of manufacture 1930s
Pattern number 4512
Backstamp 6

A pink, mother-of-pearl lustre is used to great effect on this pattern. The ground colour seems to shimmer delicately, accentuating the hand enamelled colours of the blooms. These are picked out in turquoise, white, yellow and pink enamels. The leaves are painted in green and russet. Further leaves, outlined in gilt, form the border which is additionally decorated with enamelled flower heads.

'Lakeside Flowers' (picture page 91)

Date of manufacture 1930s
Pattern number 4025
Backstamp 6

Using a ground colour of a deep burgundy red, this design is intensely dramatic. Dark-coloured trees and foliage are silhouetted starkly and form a contrasting backdrop for the plants in the foreground. These are in various shades of yellow and pink, with the leaves in green, and appear to fringe a lake, the water being picked out in black and yellow.

'Leaves' (picture page 91)

Date of manufacture 1950s
Backstamp 12

A simple, yet effective, sheet pattern of brown leaves and berries cover the tobacco jar. The ground colour is cream, with a mother-of-pearl finish.

Ming (picture page 90)

Date of manufacture 1925+
Backstamps: Bowl: Backstamp 53
          Floweraid: Backstamp 3
          Bird: Backstamp 2

This design of an oriental dragon was also used on tableware of plain ground colours in 1925 and was advertised in trade catalogues of the time in the form of cube-shaped teapots and Octagon sandwich sets. The floating bowl illustrated has a mottled ground colour of dark blue, the only ornamentation being the transfer printed cream border decorated with black oriental dragons. The lustred 'Arbor' block or Floweraid, which is contemporary with the bowl, is in the shape of a tree trunk. The bird flower holder, identified in the Grimwades catalogue as a Golden Oriole, is hand painted, but not lustred, and was intended for used with the lustre bowls and table centres. (see also Floating Bowls and Table Centres)

'Nasturtium' (picture page 91)

Date of manufacture 1930s
Backstamp 6

Vivid orange has been used in a scale design for the ground colour, which contrasts well with the mottled yellow interior rim. The nasturtium leaves are in shades of green, the flowers being in yellow, deepening to orange at the edges. The 'dragon' handle of the jug is also in orange.

'Peacock'

Date of manufacture 1925+
Backstamp 51
Impressed 5 25 which is possibly a date mark.

A flamboyant pattern which takes up almost the entire surface of the plate illustrated. The ground colour is mottled yellow against which are painted stylised scrolling branches in burgundy and a deep petrol blue. The cock bird is perched centrally and has a body colour of bright blue, his crest being picked out in pink, blue and green. The curving tail is in shades of petrol, blue and pink and the 'eyes' on the tail are in yellow, green, pink and blue.

'Petunias'

(picture page 93)

Date of manufacture 1930s
Pattern number 3097
Backstamp 6

Colourful flowers and leaves sprawl profusely over the jug illustrated. The ground colour is a pale mottled tan with an interior rim finish of lilac. The handle is dark brown and this colour is also used as an in-fill for the flowers and leaves. The blooms are portrayed in vivid yellow, deep pink, pale orange and pale pink, with accents of dark turquoise, green and purple. The leaves are in dark green, purple and pale orange, accented with tan and light green.

'Pheasant'

(picture page 93)

Date of manufacture 1930s
Pattern number 8612
Backstamp 3

A hand painted cock bird perches on a leafy branch and is depicted in naturalistic colours of russet, shaded turquoise, yellow and tan. The leaves are in autumnal colours. Unlike 'Peacock' (above), the painting is contained within the centre of the plate, allowing the lilac ground to contrast quietly. The signature b. Austin can be seen - a signature which occurs on other hand painted game bird and flower designs (see Hand Painted chapter).

'Plums'

(picture page 93)

Date of manufacture 1930s
Backstamp 3

It is unusual to find a teapot in lustre ware - the lustre being so prone to rubbing and wear that many will have been thrown away as unattractive. The dark orange lustre is a perfect foil for the purple and yellow plums. The pattern is lightened by the occasional blossom in white and the addition of blue and green leaves. The lid is decorated with buds and flowers in white and blue leaves.

'Poppies'
(picture page 94)

Date of manufacture 1930s
Backstamp 7

A simple, yet effective, design shows shaded yellow poppies against a vivid orange ground. The light and dark green leaves provide minor contrast.

'Romance'
(picture page 94)

Date of manufacture 1925+
Pattern number 5564
Backstamp 51

A colourful pattern showing a couple standing against a backdrop of water, painted an improbable yellow, with a castle perched high on a hill. Like the water, the sky is yellow, with fluffy clouds in white and lavender. Far distant hills are indigo while the cliff-top grass and that in the foreground is bright green. The girl's dress in deep pink trimmed with lilac, while the man's doublet is petrol blue. Stylised trees flank the couple and frame the scene.

'Scrolls and Flowers'
(picture page 94)

Date of manufacture 1951+
Backstamp 17

Rich burgundy is used as a ground colour for this ornate and stylised pattern. The scrolls are in gilt, as is the shell border. Groups of flowers are depicted in apricot, blue, pink, yellow and lilac. The leaves are in a soft apple green. It is a more striking and ornate pattern than was usually produced during this period.

'Shells'
(picture page 94)

Date of manufacture 1940s+

Although the candy box illustrated bears no backstamp, it was undoubtedly made at the Royal Winton factory, being of a known and identifiable shape. It is more than likely that the pattern was designed by Mabel Leigh, a talented pottery designer who made her name with the pottery manufacturers, Shorter & Son in Stoke-on-Trent. Her career is well documented in the book *The Shorter Connection* by Irene and Gordon Hopwood, and reveals that during the latter part of World War II, Mabel Leigh played a part in the export drive that was encouraged by the Government and spear-headed by Gordon Forsyth. Mabel Leigh, together with Gordon Forsyth and Eric Tunstall, were allocated studios at the Royal Winton factory. During this period, Mabel Leigh experimented with lustre ware and some fine pieces were produced. It is not known how many designs – if any – ever went into production. However, signed examples of her work, bearing the Royal Winton backstamp have been seen in a private collection and these included marine subjects such as fish and shells, identical to box illustrated.

The shells, together with sea creatures such as anemones and sea snails, are hand painted in delicate pastel colours and set against a black ground before being given a lustrous, mother-of-pearl finish. It is likely that this design was a prototype which never went into production.

'Silver Birch' (picture page 95)

Date of manufacture 1930s
Backstamp 6

Possibly, another experimental piece – the trees in the foreground appear to have transfer printed outlines, being over-painted by hand. The painting of the foliage appears rather clumsy and heavy, with dark green dominating, while the row of trees in the background is picked out in two shades of brown. The foreground is a little more delicately done and lighter colours have been used. The sky is of the typical Gobelin blue used by Royal Winton for much of their lustre ware.

'Standard Rose Bush' (picture page 95)

Date of manufacture 1930s
Pattern number 4551
Backstamp 6

A single standard rose bush, well laden with blooms, forms this design. The stylised flowers are in shades of yellow and lilac, and pale pink, dark pink, tan and lilac. Round berry-like shapes are in dark pink, yellow and blue, while the foliage is in two shades of green. Purple is used for decoration at both the base and rim, with blue delphiniums seen also at the base. The ground colour is a mottled light tan, with the inner rim done in a mottled lilac.

'Stylised Flowers' (picture page 95)

Date of manufacture 1950s
Backstamp 13

A simple pattern of two flowers, one half-opened, together with patterned leaves, is set against a plain cream ground. Beige is used for the design, the petals of the flowers being further hand painted in black and orange. A wide lustre band gives contrast.

'Summer Bouquet' (picture page 95)

Date of manufacture 1930s
Backstamp 6

A stylised bouquet of flowers and leaves is arranged against a two-tone ground of green and amber. The foliage is in two shades of green, some leaves bordered in brown, while the flowers are in tan, yellow and blue with purple, dark pink and black highlights.

'Sunburst'

(picture page 96)

Date of manufacture 1930s
Pattern number 2505
Backstamp 6

Gilt sunrays peeping out from behind gilded clouds give this pattern its name. Large stylised flower heads are painted in colours of ochre, yellow and dark pink, while the leaves are in green, turquoise, lilac and a burgundy brown. Light tan areas are decorated with white bubbles outlined in gilt, while a reversed cornucopia is striped in lilac and green with bands of petrol blue and white and flashes of yellow. The pattern contrasts vividly with the dark blue ground.

'Trees and Roses'

(picture page 96)

Date of manufacture 1930s
Pattern number 3083
Backstamp 4

Stylised flower heads, set on thorny stems, are set against a background of trees. The trees are in a deep tan with the flowers being in yellow, green, lilac, pink and blue; the stems are green. The in-fill colour between the stems and flowers is deep purple with the foreground being a light tan. Behind the trees can be seen a grey sky lightened with fluffy white clouds.

'Tudor Rose'

(picture page 96)

Date of manufacture 1930s
Backstamp 3

A stylised border of flat flower heads and leaves, together with jardinière or plant pot shapes, is set against a mottled blue ground. The flowers are either in green and white with dashes of dark red, in pale pink, or in yellow. Stamens are picked out in gilt. The jardinieres hold black-leaved plants and are ornamented with dark pink, white and yellow. All leaves are defined by gilding. This border pattern is set against a black ground and highlighted with gilt scrolls.

'Tulips'

(picture page 96)

Date of manufacture 1930s
Backstamp 7

The Spring-like appeal of this pattern is further enhanced by the use of a light green ground. Dark red and yellow tulips, with their spiky leaves, are seen accompanied by cottage garden flowers in blue and lilac.

'Trailing Harebells'

(picture page 97)

Date of manufacture 1930s
Backstamp 7

Stylised harebell-like flowers in turquoise blue and yellow enamelling trail down from a group of abstract flower heads in beige, yellow and ochre which are enhanced with bright turquoise and orange enamelling. Leaf shapes and pods are in green and grey, while an abstract clump of leaves is in green and black and highlighted with orange and yellow enamels. The pattern is set on a burgundy ground and this colour is also used on the reverse.

Watteau   (picture page 97)

Date of manufacture 1925+
Pattern number 5599
Backstamp 54

Based on scenes from paintings by the French painter, Jean Antoine Watteau (1684-1721), the Watteau pattern shows courtly figures in silhouette, promenading against a background of trees and grass picked out in grey. Figures of Pan playing his pipes are set on columns and these flank the promenaders. The ground colour is yellow, with the interior being Gobelin blue.

'Winter Flowers'   (picture page 97)

Date of manufacture 1938+
Backstamp 6

This pattern was advertised by Grimwades in October 1938, and the fly sheet shows a large ginger jar. Unfortunately, no pattern name or number was given.

The dark blue ground, edged with purple, gives dramatic impact to the design, which consists of a stylised bouquet of flowers and leaves in yellow, apricot, green, blue and dark pink, together with white buds. Further stylised branches and leaves in turquoise, green and apricot form a border on the plate illustrated. Gilt 'bubbles' help lighten the dark ground. The reverse of the plate is bright orange.

'Yellow Iris'   (picture page 97)

Date of manufacture 1930s
Backstamp 9

Yellow flag irises, accompanied by spear-like leaves in various shades of green, dominate this pattern. The dark blue ground complements the pattern and is further accentuated by the vivid orange interior colour.

Plain Colours   (picture page 98)

Date of manufacture 1925-1950s
Backstamp 51, 55

Plain colours were used a great deal for items associated with smoking, such as tobacco jars and ashtrays. These were often marketed as advertising pieces, a great many being made for Comoy's of London. Plain colours were also used for fruit bowls, flower bowls and baskets.

Orange, known by Grimwades as Tangerine, was combined with Gobelin blue, and the same blue was used in combination with yellow, with all colours having a sponged or mottled finish. This finish, together with the three colours, is instantly recognisable as coming from the Royal Winton factory, even when pieces are unmarked.

Golden Age

(picture page 98)

Date of manufacture 1950s
Backstamp 11, 13, 14

This ware was intended for customers to buy and give as gifts on wedding anniversaries. The gold lustre is particularly rich and pieces are generally covered inside and out, with the exception of flower vases. It is very prone to wear, however, and scratches easily.

Silver lustre was also made, sometimes with a hammered finish giving a pewter-like effect. Classical shapes were used, and handles on teapots were painted black.

Wide borders of gold were sometimes used as decoration on non-lustred pieces (see Stylised Flowers).

Lustre Ware Pattern Names and Numbers

Some pattern numbers are difficult to read. Where these are not clear, they have been given a question mark.

Apples	
Asters	5284
Autumn Leaves	
Dark red ground	4194
Green ground	4233
Aztec Fringe	
Bubbles	
Orange ground	4071
Green ground	5280
Butterfly	
Carnation	2322
Castle by the Lake	4581
Cherry Blossom	
Mid-blue ground	4820
Dark blue ground	10088
Cherries	
Chinese Dragon	2271?
Chrysanthemum	2134
Courtship	
Crazy Paving	
Cream ground	2258?
Pink ground	2997
Daisies	
Dragonfly	
Fairy Cobwebs	2351
Floral Bouquet	298
Fruit	7899
Fuchsia	4418
Galleon	4953
Garland	4456
Hollyhocks	
Honeysuckle	
Humming Birds	
Hydrangea	4512
Lakeside Flowers	4025
Ming	
Nasturtium	
Peacock	
Petunias	3097
Pheasant	8612
Plums	
Poppies	

Romance	5564
Scrolls and Flowers	
Shells	
Silver Birch	
Standard Rose Bush	4551
Summer Bouquet	
Sunburst	2505
Trees and Roses	3083
Tudor Rose	
Tulips	
Volcano Flowers	5316
Watteau	5599
Winter Flowers	
Yellow Iris	

Lustre Ware Pattern numbers

298	Floral Bouquet
2134	Chrysanthemum
2258?	Crazy Paving (cream)
2271?	Chinese Dragon
2322	Carnation
2351	Fairy Cobwebs
2505	Sunburst
2997	Crazy Paving (pink)
3083	Trees and Roses
3097	Petunias
4025	Lakeside Flowers
4071	Bubbles (orange ground)
4194	Autumn Leaves (dark red ground)
4233	Autumn Leaves (green ground)
4418	Fuchsia
4456?	Garland
4512	Hydrangea
4551	Standard Rose
4581	Castle by the Lake
4820	Cherry Blossom (blue ground)
4953	Galleon
5280	Bubbles (green ground)
5284	Asters
5316	Volcano Flowers
5564	Romance
5599	Watteau
7899	Fruit
8612	Pheasant
10088	Cherry Blossom (dark blue ground)

Musical Jugs, Character Jugs and Figures

MUSICAL JUGS

There is little or no information regarding these attractive jugs, apart from the fact they were made before World War II. However, manufacture continued well into the 1950s, as the backstamps confirm.

The first example mentioned in the trade papers was the tankard made in 1937 to commemorate the coronation of George VI. They were mentioned again in 1938, when *The Pottery Gazette* refers to 'Balmoral Castle', 'Stirling Castle' and 'Come to the Fair'. There is no further reference available and it is impossible to know exactly how many different varieties were made.

The jugs were fitted with a musical movement and this was protected by a gilded wooden base. All jugs originally carried a rectangular paper label which was stuck on to the wooden base, printed 'Thorens Movement, Made in Switzerland'. The name of the tune was typed on to the label and jugs are identified by collectors by these song titles. Unfortunately, many of these labels have disappeared over the years. Occasionally, an oval gilt and black label can be found, stamped 'Presenta, A Genuine Musical Novelty'.

All the tankards carry the Royal Winton backstamp, but this is often concealed beneath the musical movement.

Annie Laurie   (picture page 99)

Date of manufacture 1930s+
Backstamp 13

This features a Scotsman and his lass beside a stream. The man wears a green coat, a brown kilt and Tam o'Shanter, and carries a shepherd's crook. The girl is portrayed seated, wearing a red dress, and holding a yellow shawl over her head. The background consists of green and heather-clad hills, while on the reverse of the jug, the stream widens and is spanned by a small bridge. The handle is topped by a thistle flower.

Come to the Fair   (picture page 99)

Date of manufacture 1930s+
Backstamp 13

Mentioned by *The Pottery Gazette* in February 1938, the jug is perhaps one of the most attractive in the series. A balloon seller, clad in a dark green coat, brown breeches, and wearing a black hat, can be seen sitting on a hill overlooking a fairground. He clutches a large bunch of balloons, picked out in pastel colours of blue, yellow and pink. The fairground scene shows a merry-go-round, complete with horses and riders, with a striped cover in dark pink and yellow; a swing-boat and covered tent are in the background. Crowds of people can be seen in front of booths which are striped in yellow and blue. The handle of the jug resembles the trunk of a tree.

Floral Dance

(picture page 99)

Date of manufacture 1930s+
Backstamp 6

A trio of two men and a woman are seen dancing with linked hands in front of a cottage and along a cobbled street. The men wear pink and green coats, yellow breeches and blue and green knee length socks. The woman wears a yellow dress with a blue trim and a green hat.

The reverse of the jug shows a village street with attractive three-storey houses, flanked by trees and a wooden fence. The handle of the jug appears to jut out from a wall or pillar and consists of some of the musical instruments mentioned in the song.

George VI Coronation

(picture page 99)

Date of manufacture 1937

A Royal Winton advertisement, dating from 1937, assured buyers that, 'The beer or cider tankard is a beautiful specimen of Pottery Handcraft. Relief modelled, hand-painted in Royal colours, with burnished gold finish'.

The tankards were available with or without musical fittings at a cost of 15/- (75p) or 9/6d (47½p) respectively. There was a choice of tunes, too, either 'God Save the King' or 'Here's a Health (Unto His Majesty)'.

Queen Mary ordered 5 tankards on the 5th April 1937, choosing the tune 'God Save the King'.

The tankard was modelled by Percy Lloyd and features King George VI and Queen Elizabeth, shown in profile, enclosed in a laurel wreath surmounted by a crown. Below are the flowers of Great Britain and the intertwined initials GR.

The reverse portrays the coat of arms of the country with a ribbon reading 'George VI Coronation May 12th 1937'. The handle is formed from flowers and leaves, and topped with a crown.

Killarney

(picture page 100)

Date of manufacture 1930s+
Backstamp 6

Mountains in shadowy blues and pinks overlook a lake, which appears to be spanned by a bridge. A man in a rowing boat casts his line into the water. The foreground features rocks, grass and flowers, while the reverse shows a leafy tree. The handle is formed by a man, who wears a dark green coat, yellow breeches and dark pink gaiters. His hat is brown and he holds a red kerchief to his mouth.

Phil the Fluters Ball (picture page 100))

Date of manufacture 1930s+
Backstamp 13, 58

A lively scene of dancers is portrayed in rather subdued colours of tan, beige, dark green, dark brown, grey, yellow, pink and maroon on a plain cream ground. A group of four dancers can be seen, clasping hands in a circle. Two musicians play the drum and the flute in the background. To one side, a stool supports two bottles and a beer mug, while on the other side, a small pink pig is dancing on his hind legs. Above, festive streamers and balloons complete the merry picture.

The reverse of the jug shows the exterior of the thatched house or pub set against a background of pale purple hills, with a lady driving a jaunting car towards it. She wears a pink dress with a white, ruffled collar and a pink hat trimmed with bright yellow flowers. She has one hand on the reins and encourages the donkey with a whip. The handle is plain.

Sarie Marais (picture page 100)

Date of manufacture 1930s+
Backstamp 6

This shows a South African scene with a couple trekking across the veldt in their covered wagon which is drawn by a team of oxen yoked together. Muted creams, yellows, and beiges are used, the only touches of colour coming from the woman's pink dress, the man's blue coat and a small amount of green grass in the foreground.

The team of oxen continues on to the reverse, and is led by a man in a bright green coat, carrying a whip, and this whip also forms the handle of the jug.

The tune Sarie Marais is of South African origin.

Stirling Castle (picture page 100)

Date of manufacture 1930s+
Backstamp 13

One of the few jugs to carry an inscription. The castle is portrayed in soft yellows, while the cliffs and foliage are in blue and green. The reverse shows pale pink hills, blue water, trees and grass, and is also inscribed with the word 'Tarbet'. The handle is formed by intertwined bagpipes and thistles.

The tune is 'Road to the Isles'.

There is a Tavern in the Town (picture page 100)

Date of manufacture 1930s+
Backstamp 13

A public house scene is featured with a merry gentleman in a white wig dandling a young woman on his knee, while the landlord surreptitiously fills his tankard. The man wears a pink coat, white cravat and green waistcoat. His knee breeches are plum coloured. The woman holds a glass aloft and wears a low cut dress in tan with a white ruffled neckline, while the landlord wears a green shirt, white apron and green stockings. All three wear black, buckled shoes.

The interior of the inn has blue mullioned windows, a tripod table, complete with beer tankards, and a brown wooden settle. A black cat surveys the scene.

The reverse of the jug shows the outside of the pub with its bay window, and a wooden seat. A tree stands on the grass which is fronted with pink flowers. The name of the pub, Ye Swan Inn, is seen on a board that is suspended on a wooden post.

Under the Spreading Chestnut Tree   (picture page 100)

Date of manufacture 1930s+
Backstamp 6

A country couple sit clasping hands outside a house, she perched on his knee, under the leafy shade of a chestnut tree. A white dove is perched in the tree above their heads. The brickwork of the house is well defined and the leaded windows are picked out in dark blue. The girl wears a blue dress with a white collar while her yokel lover wears a cream coloured smock. Both are wearing shady white hats banded in red.

The reverse of the jug shows an arched gate leading into a farmyard, complete with farm machinery. The words of the song are printed below the branches of the chestnut:

> 'Underneath the Spreading Chestnut tree
> I loved her and she loved me
> There she used to sit upon my knee
> Neath the Spreading Chestnut tree'

The handle of the jug is formed by the tree.

CHARACTER JUGS

These were produced in the late 1930s and many were based on wartime personalities. They are of excellent quality, and were superbly modelled by Billy Grindy, a talented man who was exempt from fighting in World War II by being in a reserved occupation. After the war, Mr Grindy moved on to Thomas C. Wild & Sons Ltd (Royal Albert) where he designed the Montreaux shape for the Royal Albert pattern 'Country Roses'. He also worked for Shaw & Copestake Ltd, where he modelled the toby jugs that were issued under the Sylvac backstamp.

Again, a complete listing of the character jugs made is not available, but it is known that the following jugs featuring wartime persona were produced: Winston Churchill, George VI (in uniform), General Douglas MacArthur, Field Marshal Jan Smuts, Franklin D. Roosevelt and General Sir Archibald Wavell. Patriotically, John Bull and Uncle Sam were also portrayed. The character jugs appear to have been made in three or possibly four sizes, ranging from 3 inches to 7 inches. Identifying names are printed above the backstamp.

Non-military character jugs were manufactured, some in the Dickens series which was first introduced in 1931 (see Figures). Those found so far include, Mr Pickwick, Mr Winkle and a non-Dickens Indian Chief. The Dickens series would appear to have been made to hold liquor, rather than to be character jugs, as there is no opening other than a round hole fitted with a corked metal stopper. This is sometimes at the front of the piece, on top, sometimes at the back. They can also be found, identically modelled and coloured, with a Kelsboro backstamp instead of a Royal Winton backstamp, but the reason behind this discrepancy is not known. The names of the Dickens characters are impressed on the reverse of the piece.

General Douglas Macarthur   (picture page 101)

Date of manufacture late 1930s+
Backstamp 56

MacArthur wears the American uniform with US in yellow on his collar and a star on his epaulettes. His hat features the American eagle, and is banded with gold braid, with gold braid also on the peak. An unsheathed sword forms the handle.

General Sir Archibald Wavell   (picture page 102)

Date of manufacture late 1930s+
Backstamp as 56

The General is portrayed in khaki uniform with red and yellow tabs on his collar. His hat is banded with red and is decorated with gold braid and a regimental insignia. The handle of the jug is formed by an unsheathed sword.

John Bull   (picture page 101)

Date of manufacture 1930s+
Backstamp 7

The symbol of England, John Bull wears a dark green hunting coat, a high collar and a red cravat tied in a bow, together with a black top hat. The hand is formed by a riding crop.

Indian Chief   (picture page 102)

Date of manufacture 1930s+
Backstamp 7

A native American is shown wearing a feathered war bonnet, additionally decorated with banding and beading. The feathers are yellow and brown with red and blue tips. The head band is red, yellow and green, the strips of beading being blue, red and yellow. The handle of the jug is formed from feathers.

Pickwick

(picture page 102)

Date of manufacture 1930s+
Backstamp 7

Mr Pickwick presents a cheerful face as he smiles and peers over his spectacles. His coat is blue and he wears a yellow kerchief below his wing collar. A flat hat in dark green completes the picture. The handle consists of a furled umbrella.

Uncle Sam

(picture page 101)

Date of manufacture late 1930s+
Backstamp 7

The character bears a marked resemblance to Abraham Lincoln and wears a dark green coat with a wing collar with a floppy brown cravat tied in a bow. He has grey collar-length hair, heavy eyebrows and a jutting-out beard. He wears a grey top hat banded with blue and spaced with white stars. On larger figures, the handle is made from dollar signs.

FIGURES

The Dickens series of figures was introduced in the early 1930s and the first mention appears in *The Pottery Gazette* in October 1931 when a photograph of bookends was published. A contemporary catalogue shows that the series of 6 figures produced consisted of Pickwick, Sam Weller, Bumble, Micawber, Pecksniff and Sairey Gamp. The complete set, in a box, was priced at 36/- (£1.80).

The modelling is crisp and the hand painted colours are strong and vivid, although the quality of the painting can and does vary.

A series of figures was produced by Grimwades, issued under the Atlas China backstamp between 1936-38 and these are more romantically inclined. Unfortunately, no documentation exists at all in relation to these, and they are so rarely found that it is possible they were made for export only. However, it is known that the following were produced, Pan, Playmates, Bathing Belle, Dutch Girl, Jester, Pierrot and Masquerade.

Two figure groups have been discovered which are identical in colouring and modelling, apart from a slight tilt of the girl's head which could have occurred during the piecing together of the figure. These have different names printed on the base; one is called Romance, the other A Token of Love. The titles are painted on by hand, so it possible that an error was made at that stage.

Mr Bumble (bookends)

(picture page 103)

Date of manufacture 1931+
Backstamp 57

This Dickens character of a tipstaff wears a dark grey caped coat, bound with dark pink, with a matching pink waistcoat. The buttons are yellow. His cockaded hat is dark grey with a yellow border. He carries a staff in his left hand.

Mr Bumble (picture page 103)

Date of manufacture 1931+
Backstamp 1

The Mr Bumble figure appears to have been made from the same mould as the bookends (above).

Sairey Gamp (picture page 103)

Date of manufacture 1931+
Backstamp 1

The laundress is portrayed clutching a furled umbrella while carrying her bundle of washing. She wears a brightly painted shawl in dark pink, patterned in blue, green and yellow, over a black skirt. Her black bonnet has a yellow ribbon. Her laundry bundle is yellow with a brown design and her umbrella is dark green.

Masquerade (picture page 104)

Date of manufacture 1936/38+
Backstamp 59

The girl portrayed wears a low cut ball gown with ruffles at the square neckline and a ruff around her neck. She carries a fan in one hand and a mask in the other. Her dress is a purplish indigo and splashed with large pink flowers.

Romance and A Token of Love (picture page 104)

Date of manufacture 1936/38+
Backstamp as 59

These figures are virtually identical, the only differences being the tilt of the girl's head and the title written on the base. As these models were made in sections, then assembled, it is easy to see how differences could occur.

The girl's low cut dress is delicately shaded in pink and blue and closely resembles that worn by Masquerade (above). Her companion wears a pink coat, a yellow waistcoat and blue breeches. His buckled shoes are pink.

Price Guide

Perhaps the most difficult part of a book to write or compile is the section headed 'Price Guide'. Every collector wants to know how much to pay for things or what a given item in their collection is worth.

Prices are highly subjective; one collector may scoff at the price asked by a dealer, while another must have the piece at any cost. An old saying in the antiques trade maintains that something is worth just what someone is prepared to pay for it, and that saying holds true.

The following price guide is exactly that – a guide. Prices can, and do, vary considerably. If a dealer has bought cheaply, he might pass that saving on to the customer; another dealer may have paid far more for an identical piece and this will be reflected in the asking price. There are regional, national and international variations, too, and if items are fetching more money in other countries, then prices go up in the United Kingdom.

Differences in prices between apparently similar designs in a series may puzzle some collectors. But some patterns or colourways are more desirable than others and competition is fierce, thus increasing prices. Also, some patterns are more rare than others and this, too, will have an effect.

Minimum and maximum prices are shown in the guide, but these refer to items in perfect condition. Restoration, chips and cracks will devalue a piece, as will rubbing or wear on lustre.

It has been possible to give a comprehensive listing for some of the patterns, such as Rosebud, for example, as contemporary catalogue pages indicate what was available and pieces can still be found today. However, there is a paucity of information on some ranges, so prices have been given only on items illustrated, items known to have been manufactured, or items that would fetch similar prices in the same shape, regardless of pattern.

The only i that is unpriced is the lustre candy box of 'Shells' design. As it is believed to have been an experimental piece, its value cannot be estimated.

COTTAGE WARE

	Anne Hathaway's Cottage		Olde England	
Biscuit Barrels	£100-£150	$180-$270	£60-£90	$110-$165
Butter dishes	£60-£90	$110-$165	£40-£50	$70-$90
Cheese dishes	£120-£180	$215-$325	£50-£80	$90-$145
Condiments 4-piece	£60-£95	$110-$170	£50-£70	$90-$125
Cruets 3-piece	£50-£80	$90-$145	£30-£50	$55-$90
Dessert plates	£45-£75	$80-$135	£45-£60	$80-$110
Sugar shakers	£40-£80	$70-$145	£40-£70	$70-$125
Teapots	£150-£250	$270-$450	£120-£160	$215-$290

Ye Olde Inne

	(Red roof)		(Grey roof)	
Biscuit Barrels	£75-£100	$135-$180	£100-£150	$180-$270
Butter dishes	£50-£80	$90-$145	£70-£90	$125-$165
Cheese dishes	£75-£100	$135-$180	£80-£140	$145-$250
Condiments 4-piece	£50-£70	$90-$125	£70-£90	$125-$165
Cruets 3-piece	£45-£60	$80-$110	£50-£70	$90-$125
Dessert plates	——	——	£45-£75	$80-$135
Jugs: Cream	£40-£60	$70-$110	£50-£85	$90-$155
Jugs: Hot water	£60-£90	$110-$165	£75-£100	$135-$180
Preserve pots	£35-£55	$60-$100	£45-£70	$80-$125
Sugar shakers	£45-£75	$80-$135	£60-£90	$110-$165
Teapots	£60-£100	$110-$180	£80-£150	$145-$270
4-piece teasets (Premium)	£150-£280	$270-$505	——	——

Ye Olde Mill

	(Red roof)		(Pink roof)	
Biscuit Barrels	£80-£120	$145-$215	£120-£175	$215-$315
Butter dishes	£50-£70	$90-$125	£80-£100	$145-$180
Cheese dishes	£75-£95	$135-$170	£100-£150	$180-$270
Condiments 4-piece	£60-£80	$110-$145	£80-£100	$145-$180
Cruets 3-piece	£40-£60	$70-$110	£55-£90	$100-$165
Cups & saucers	——	——	£50-£80	$90-$145
Dessert plates	——	——	£50-£80	$90-$145
Jugs: Hot water	£60-£90	$110-$165	£80-£120	$145-$215
Jugs: Cream	£35-£50	$60-$90	£50-£80	$90-$145
Sugar shakers	£40-£70	$70-$125	£60-£100	$110-$180
Teapots	£80-£150	$145-$270	£150-£250	$270-$450

Shakespeare's Birthplace   Dessert Plates   £50-£80 $90-$145

RELIEF MOULDED WARE

	Beehive		Chanticleer	
Biscuit Barrels	£120-£180	$215-$325	——	——
Butter dishes	£80-£120	$145-$215	£80-£100	$145-$180
Cheese dishes	£120-£180	$215-$325	£100-£150	$180-$270
Condiments 4-piece	£70-£100	$125-$180	£60-£90	$110-$165
Cruets 3-piece	£55-£80	$100-$145	£50-£70	$90-$125
Dessert plates	£50-£80	$90-$145	——	——
Jugs: Cream	£50-£75	$90-$135	£45-£70	$80-$125
Jugs: Milk	——	——	£60-£90	$110-$165
Preserve pots	£50-£90	$90-$165	£60-£90	$110-$165
Sugar bowls	£40-£55	$70-$100	£40-£55	$70-$100
Sugar shakers	£70-£100	$125-$180	£60-£90	$110-$165
Teapots	£250-£300	$450-$540		
(Blue)			£80-£120	$145-$215
(Brown)			£150-£200	$270-$360
Toast racks:				
3-bar	£50-£70	$90-$125	£50-£80	$90-$145
5-bar	£65-£90	$115-$165	£70-£95	$125-$170

Castle on the Hill   Cheese dishes   £100-£150 $180-$270

Countryside   Sweetmeat dishes   £50-£75 $90-$135

Crocus	Sundae dishes	£35-£55	$60-$100
	Sugar shakers	£40-£70	$70-$125
Dovecote	Fruit bowls	£70-£100	$125-$180
	Vases TAME shape	£70-£100	$125-$180
Galleon	Biscuit boxes	£65-£100	$115-$180
Game (Dark Blue)	Biscuit barrels	£60-£100	$110-$180
	Dessert plates	£45-£70	$80-$125
	Preserve pots	£35-£50	$60-$90
	Sugar shakers	£40-£70	$70-$125
Game (Cream)	Vases TIBER shape	£50-£80	$90-$145

	Gera		Lakeland	
Cheese dishes	£80-£120	$145-$215	£100-£150	$180-$270
Condiments 4-piece	£60-£90	$110-$165	£75-£95	$135-$170
Cruets 3-piece	£45-£65	$80-$115	£50-£70	$90-$125
Dessert plates	£45-£65	$80-$115	£45-£70	$80-$125
Fruit Bowls	£65-£90	$115-$165	£150-£200	$270-$360
Jugs: Cream	£40-£60	$70-$110	£50-£70	$90-$125
Jugs: Hot water	£70-£100	$125-$180	£100-£150	$180-$270
Jugs: Milk	£40-£75	$70-$135	£80-£120	$145-$215
Mint boats + stands	£40-£55	$70-$100	£40-£60	$70-$110
Preserve pots	£45-£65	$80-$115	£50-£70	$90-$125
Sugar bowls	£30-£45	$55-$80	£30-£45	$55-$80
Sugar shakers	£50-£80	$90-$145	£60-£80	$110-$145
Tea plates	£30-£45	$55-$80	£30-£40	$55-$70
Teapots	£100-£150	$180-$270	£150-£250	$270-$450
Toast racks:				
3-bar	£40-£60	$70-$110	£50-£75	$90-$135
5-bar	£50-£80	$90-$145	£75-£100	$135-$180
Twin Trays	£40-£65	$70-$115	£50-£75	$90-$135

Haystack	Teapots	£150-£200	$270-$360
Iris	Tall vase	£200-£250	$360-$450
Pagoda	Condiments 4-piece	£60-£90	$110-$165
	Cruets 3-piece	£50-£75	$90-$135
	Sugar shakers	£60-£90	$110-$165
	Toast racks: 3-bar	£45-£65	$80-$115
	Toast racks: 5-bar	£60-£90	$110-$165
	Twin trays (small)	£40-£60	$70-$110
Peony	Cheese dishes	£100-£150	$180-$270
	Condiments 4-piece	£60-£90	$110-$165
	Cruets 3-piece	£50-£70	$90-$125
	Dessert plates	£45-£70	$80-$125
	Jugs: Cream	£40-£60	$70-$110
	Muffin dishes	£70-£100	$125-$180
	Preserve pots	£40-£60	$70-$110
	Sugar bowls	£30-£40	$55-$70
	Sugar shakers	£50-£75	$90-$135
	Teapots	£150-£200	$270-$360
	Toast racks: 3-bar	£40-£60	$70-$110
	Toast racks: 5-bar	£50-£80	$90-$145

Pixie

Item	£	$
Cheese dishes	£90-£150	$165-$270
Condiments 4-piece	£60-£90	$110-$165
Cruets 3-piece	£50-£70	$90-$125
Dessert plates	£45-£65	$80-$115
Jugs: Cream	£30-£50	$55-$90
Jugs: Hot water	£80-£120	$145-$215
Jugs: Milk	£60-£85	$110-$155
Jugs: Flower	£100-£150	$180-$270
Mint boats + stands	£35-£50	$60-$90
Preserve pots	£45-£65	$80-$115
Sugar bowls	£30-£50	$55-$90
Sugar shakers	£75-£95	$135-$170
Teapots	£150-£200	$270-$360
Toast racks: 3-bar	£50-£70	$90-$125
Toast racks: 5-bar	£65-£95	$115-$170
Wall clocks	£100-£150	$180-$270

	Primula		Regina	
Biscuit Barrels	£60-£90	$110-$165	£60-£95	$110-$170
Cheese dishes	£50-£80	$90-$145	£50-£80	$90-$145
Comports	£40-£60	$70-$110	£40-£60	$70-$110
Condiments 4-piece	£45-£70	$80-$125	£40-£60	$70-$110
Cruets 3-piece	£35-£55	$60-$100	£40-£65	$70-$115
Egg Sets	£45-£65	$80-$110	£45-£60	$80-$110
Dessert plates	£30-£50	$55-$90	£30-£50	$55-$90
Fruit/salad bowls	£40-£70	$70-$125	£40-£65	$70-$115
Jugs: Cream	£30-£45	$55-$80	£30-£45	$55-$80
Jugs: Hot water	£60-£85	$110-$155	£65-£85	$115-$155
Jugs: Milk	£40-£60	$70-$110	£40-£60	$70-$110
Mint boats + stands	£40-£60	$70-$110	£40-£60	$70-$110
Preserve pots	£35-£55	$60-$100	£35-£60	$60-$110
Sugar bowls	£25-£40	$45-$70	£25-£45	$45-$80
Sugar shakers	£40-£70	$70-$125	£40-£70	$70-$125
Teapots	£100-£150	$180-$270	£100-£150	$180-$270
Toast racks:				
3-bar	£40-£60	$70-$110	£40-£60	$70-$110
5-bar	£50-£70	$90-$125	£50-£70	$90-$125

Salad

Item	£	$
Bowls	£35-£60	$60-$110
Rhubarb dishes	£20-£40	$35-$70
Serving dishes	£30-£50	$55-$90
Serving trays	£30-£50	$55-$90

Terrace

Item	£	$
Chargers	£250-£350	$450-$630
Condiments 4-piece	£60-£95	$110-$170
Cruets 3-piece	£45-£70	$80-$125
Dessert plates	£45-£70	$80-$125
Preserve pots	£40-£60	$70-$110
Vase: small	£70-£100	$125-$180
Vase: medium	£80-£120	$145-$215
Vase: large	£100-£150	$180-$270

Trellis Rose Garden

Item	£	$
Biscuit barrels	£150-£200	$270-$360
Condiments 4-piece	£70-£100	$125-$180
Cruets 3-piece	£50-£75	$90-$135
Dessert plates	£50-£85	$90-$155
Jugs: Cream	£60-£80	$110-$145

Trellis Rose Garden	Jugs: Milk	£80-£120	$145-$215
	Preserve pots	£50-£80	$90-$145
	Sugar shakers	£60-£95	$110-$170
	Teapots	£200-£300	$360-$540
	Toast racks: 3-bar	£45-£65	$80-$115
	Toast racks: 5-bar	£65-£90	$115-$165
Preserve pots	Apple	£40-£60	$70-$110
	Grapes	£40-£60	$70-$110
	Lotus	£30-£55	$55-$100
	Wishing Well	£30-£50	$55-$90

PASTELS

Apple	Hors d'oeuvre dish	£40-£60	$70-$110
Apple Blossom	Fruit bowl	£40-£60	$70-$110
Briar	Condiments 4-piece	£50-£70	$90-$125
	Cruets 3-piece	£40-£60	$70-$110
	Dishes: small	£25-£40	$45-$70
	Dishes: medium	£35-£50	$60-$90
	Dishes: large	£40-£65	$70-$115
	Sugar shakers	£35-£65	$60-$115
	Toast racks: 3-bar	£45-£55	$80-$100
	Toast racks: 5-bar	£50-£75	$90-$135
	Twin trays	£25-£40	$45-$70
Fuchsia	Dishes: small	£25-£40	$45-$70
	Dishes: medium	£35-£50	$60-$90
	Dishes: large	£45-£75	$80-$135
	Mint boats + stands	£35-£50	$60-$90
	Pin trays	£15-£20	$25-$35

COMPOSITE PRICE GUIDE
Honey Lily (Tiger Lily), Hibiscus, Petunia, Rosebud

Bedside sets	£300-£500	$540-$900
Bon-bon dishes	£40-£60	$70-$110
Butter dishes	£60-£90	$110-$165
Candlesticks (pair)	£40-£75	$70-$135
Cheese dishes	£80-£120	$145-$215
Chocolate comports	£60-£90	$110-$165
Coffee pots: small	£90-£140	$165-$250
Coffee pots: large	£120-£175	$215-$315
Condiments 4-piece	£60-£90	$110-$165
Cruets 3-piece	£45-£65	$80-$115
Cups and saucers	£30-£50	$55-$90
Dressing table/trinket sets	£150-£300	$270-$540
Jugs: cream	£40-£60	$70-$110
Jugs: milk	£70-£100	$125-$180
Mint boats + stands	£40-£75	$70-$70
Plates: bread and butter	£25-£40	$45-$70
Plates: dinner	£20-£30	$35-$55
Plates: salad	£18-£28	$35-$55
Plates: tea	£12-£15	$20-$25
Preserve pots	£45-£60	$80-$110
Salad bowls	£45-£65	$80-$115
Salad bowls with servers	£70-£100	$125-$180
Sugar bowls	£20-£30	$35-$55
Sugar/cream sets	£60-£90	$110-$165

Honey Lily (Tiger Lily), Hibiscus, Petunia, Rosebud

Teapots: small		£100-£150	$180-$270
Teapots: large		£150-£250	$270-$450
Tea sets 6-place inc. teapot		£500-£700	$900-$1260
Tennis sets		£45-£60	$80-$110
Toastracks: 3-bar		£40-£60	$70-$110
Toastracks: 5-bar		£50-£75	$90-$135
Trinket pots		£30-£45	$55-$80
Wall pockets		£90-£150	$165-$270
Tea Rose	Candy Boxes	£50-£80	$90-$145
	Candlesticks	£30-£50	$55-$90
	Fruit bowls	£45-£60	$80-$110
	Wall Pockets	£80-£120	$145-$215
Plain colours	Wall clocks	£50-£75	$90-$135
Mottled ware	Canoes	£30-£50	$55-$90
	Wall pockets NITA shape	£60-£90	$110-$165
	Wall pockets ROSA shape	£70-£100	$125-$180

HAND PAINTED WARE

Delphinium	Large dished plaques	£250-£400	$450-$720
Galleon	Table lamps	£70-£95	$125-$170
Poplars	REMUS jugs	£150-£250	$270-$450
Red Roof	Plates, hand painted	£40-£60	$70-$110
	Plates, transfer printed	£20-£30	$35-$55
'6742'	Biscuit barrels	£75-£95	$135-$170
	Large dished plaques	£250-£400	$450-$720
	Plates, transfer printed	£30-£45	$55-$80
Anemone	Dishes, small oval	£40-£55	$70-$100
	Coffee sets 6-place	£400-£600	$720-$1080
Roses	Candy boxes	£70-£90	$125-$165
	Lamp bases	£150-£200	$270-$360
Fruit	Baskets KEW shape	£70-£90	$125-$165
	Jugs	£40-£75	$70-$135
Game Birds	Tobacco jars	£60-£90	$110-$165

ART DECO WARE

Blocks	Cups and saucers	£40-£60	$70-$110
Chimneys	Bedside sets	£350-£450	$630-$630
Dehli	Oblong plates	£150-£200	$270-$360
	Teapots	£200-£300	$360-$540
Flames	Baskets HAMPTON shape	£60-£85	$110-$155
	Jugs: CAMBRIDGE shape	£100-£150	$180-$270
	Jugs: Hot water GREEK shape	£100-£150	$180-$270
	Sweetmeat dishes	£60-£85	$110-$155
	Tea plates	£35-£55	$60-$100
Geometric Tulips	Jugs GLOBE shape	£100-£150	$180-$270
	Tea plates	£35-£55	$60-$100
Jazz	Coffee sets 6-place	£300-£450	$540-$630

		£	$
Jigsaw	Cream/sugar sets		
	HECTOR shape	£50-£70	$90-$125
Polka Dot	Bedside sets	£150-£250	$270-$450
	Condiments TREFOIL shape	£50-£75	$90-$135
Red Roof House (Atlas China)	Coffee cups and saucers	£30-£50	$55-$90
Tulips	Chocolate comports	£70-£100	$125-$180
Wheels	Small pots	£25-£40	$45-$70

LUSTRE WARE	**Bubbles (Orange)**		**Bubbles (Green)**	
Fruit Bowls	£60-£95	$110-$170	£40-£65	$70-$115
Ginger jars	£120-£180	$215-$325	£80-£120	$145-$215
Plates: ASCOT	£35-£60	$60-$110	£30-£50	$55-$90
Vases: small	£40-£70	$70-$125	£35-£55	$60-$100
Vases: medium	£70-£100	$125-$180	£50-£70	$90-$125
Vases: large	£100-£150	$180-$270	£70-£90	$125-$165

	Carnation		**Fairy Cobwebs**	
Biscuit boxes	£70-£95	$125-$170		
Cake plates (handled)	£35-£50	$60-$90	£40-£75	$70-$135
Plates: ASCOT	£35-£50	$60-$90	£40-£75	$70-$135
Vases: small	£40-£60	$70-$110	£70-£95	$125-$170
Vases: medium	£60-£90	$110-$165	£90-£120	$165-$215
Vases: large	£90-£150	$165-$270	£120-£175	$215-$315

Lustre (all patterns)

	£	$
Baskets ESSEX shape	£90-£150	$165-$270
Birds and Floweraids	£30-£60	$55-$110
Biscuit barrels	£60-£120	$110-$215
Bowls: medium	£50-£80	$90-$145
Bowls: large	£80-£120	$145-$215
Bowls: extra large	£100-£180	$180-$325
Cakestands	£40-£80	$70-$145
Candy Boxes	£50-£90	$90-$165
Chamber pots	£40-£90	$70-$165
Comports	£50-£90	$90-$165
Covered vases: small	£50-£90	$90-$165
Covered vases: large	£100-£200	$180-$360
Floating bowls	£50-£90	$90-$165
Floating bowls with Floweraids/birds	£80-£150	$145-$270
Jardinières	£150-£250	$270-$450
Jugs: Globe	£60-£100	$110-$180
Jugs: Remus	£150-£250	$270-$450
Jugs: Ronda	£150-£250	$270-$450
Nut dishes	£30-£50	$55-$90
Plates ASCOT + OCTAGON shape	£40-£75	$70-$135
Pot Pourri jars	£60-£90	$110-$165
Sandwich sets	£100-£200	$180-$360
Shaving mugs	£50-£75	$90-$135
Sugar shakers	£50-£90	$90-$165
Table centres	£100-£180	$180-$325
Teapots:	£90-£150	$165-$270
Tea plates	£25-£35	$45-$60
Tobacco jars	£50-£90	$90-$165
Vases: AVON shape	£40-£75	$70-$135

Lustre (all patterns)
Vases: BOUQUET shape	£60-£100	$110-$180
Vases: CAPRI shape	£40-£75	$70-$135
Vases: CINTRA shape	£60-£100	$110-$180
Vases: REMUS	£150-£250	$270-$450
Vases: VIENNA	£40-£75	$70-$135
Wall pockets	£80-£150	$145-$270

Plain colours:
Ashtrays	£15-£30	$25-$55
Fruit bowls	£30-£50	$55-$90
Jardinières	£40-£75	$70-$135
Tobacco jars	£40-£80	$70-$145
Vases	£30-£60	$55-$110
Wall pockets	£50-£80	$90-$145

Golden Age Lustre
Cake plates	£20-£30	$35-$55
Cream/sugar sets	£30-£50	$55-$90
Cups and saucers	£20-£30	$35-$55
Tea plates	£15-£20	$25-$35
Teapots	£50-£90	$90-$165
Vases: small	£30-£50	$55-$90
Vases: medium	£40-£60	$70-$110
Vases: large	£60-£90	$110-$165

MUSICAL JUGS, FIGURES AND CHARACTER JUGS etc
Musical Jugs
Annie Laurie	£150-£200	$270-$360
Come to the Fair	£175-£250	$315-$450
Floral Dance	£120-£200	$215-$360
Killarney	£120-£200	$215-$360
Phil the Fluters Ball	£120-£200	$215-$360
Sarie Marais	£180-£250	$325-$450
Stirling Castle	£100-£180	$180-$325
There is a Tavern in the Town	£120-£200	$215-$360
Under the Spreading Chestnut Tree	£130-£250	$235-$450

Character Jugs

	Small		Medium		Large	
Indian Chief	£60-£90	$110-$165	£90-£150	$165-$270	£150-£250	$270-$450
John Bull	£40-£70	$70-$125	£60-£100	$110-$180	£100-£200	$180-$360
General Douglas						
MacArthur	£60-£90	$110-$165	£80-£120	$145-$215	£150-£250	$270-$450
Uncle Sam	£40-£60	$70-$110	£50-£70	$90-$125	£80-£120	$145-$215
Sir Archibald						
Wavell	£60-£90	$110-$165	£80-£120	$145-$215	£150-£250	$270-$450

Dickens Character Heads
	Pickwick	£30-£60	$55-$110

Dickens Figures
	Bumble	£50-£75	$90-$135
	Micawber	£50-£75	$90-$135
	Pecksniff	£50-£75	$90-$135
	Pickwick	£50-£75	$90-$135
	Sairey Gamp	£50-£75	$90-$135
	Sam Weller	£50-£75	$90-$135
	Bookends	£80-£120	$145-$215

Figures
	A Token of Love	£150-£250	$270-$450
	Masquerade	£120-£200	$215-$360
	Romance	£150-£250	$270-$450

Backstamps

Although backstamps are regarded as a reliable guide to dating ceramics, it has to be borne in mind that there was a certain amount of overlapping date-wise. Manufacturers did not realise that their goods would one day become sought after and that collectors would want to know exactly when an item was made. Workers would often use whatever backstamp was to hand. One therefore finds anomalies.

For example, an early Grimwade Brothers backstamp was still being used on their ware and in their advertising as late as 1917, despite the fact that the company had changed its name to Grimwades Ltd in 1900.

The study of contemporary catalogues and trade papers sometimes gives a clue as to when a pattern, design or range of ware was produced – but there is never any mention of how long a range remained in production. Musical jugs, for example, were known to have been made prior to World War II, and were mentioned in *The Pottery Gazette* in 1937. However, a jug mentioned in the same trade paper in 1938 has been found with a backstamp dating from the 1950s. In addition, *The Pottery Gazette Year Book* for 1948 shows the typical round Art deco mark for Royal Winton (Backstamp 6) but also shows the globe mark with a Grimwades strap (Backstamp 1)

It was originally thought that the prefix Royal was added to the Winton trade name in the 1930s. However, research has shown that Royal Winton ware was being made as early as 1897 (See chapter on Products). The name was again used briefly in 1917/18, and revived in about 1929, when Grimwades introduced their new Royal Winton Ivory.

In 1942, as a result of World War II, potteries were divided into various categories and were designated a letter of the alphabet (A, B and C) with which to mark their wares, with the letters BY, CY and CZ being introduced in 1945. The letter had to be stamped indelibly under the glaze and the ruling was in force for quite a few years after the end of the war.

Grimwades were given the letter 'A' and this can be found with both the Art Deco style and Script backstamps. It is often incorporated into the backstamp and can vary in size.

There are other marks of importance to be found on the base of Royal Winton pottery. Pattern numbers, usually consisting of four-figure numbers, were hand painted, making them difficult to decipher at times. Pattern names were sometimes transfer printed near the backstamp. Any name impressed in the base is the shape name and not the pattern name, the exception being some of the pastel patterns which used the same name for both categories.

1. *1930+ Globe with GRIMWADES strap and STOKE ON TRENT ENGLAND.*

2. *1930+ Globe with GRIMWADES strap. 'WINTON WARE' above, ENGLAND below.*

3. *1930+ Globe with GRIMWADES strap. 'ROYAL WINTON' above, ENGLAND below.*

4. *1930+ ROYAL WINTON IVORY with GRIMWADES above, ENGLAND below (both curved).*

5. *1930+ ROYAL WINTON curved above IVORY.*

6. *1934+ Round Art Deco mark with GRIMWADES ENGLAND.*

7. *1934+ Round Art Deco mark with GRIMWADES MADE IN ENGLAND.*

8. *1934+ Round Art Deco mark with GRIMWADES MADE IN ENGLAND below. Sometimes overlapping is MADE IN above curved ENGLAND.*

9. *1934+ MADE IN above ENGLAND curved.*

10. *1935. Grimwades paper label for 1935.*

11. *1942+ Round Art Deco mark with GRIMWADES MADE IN ENGLAND and letter A at the base of the mark.*

12. *1942+ Royal above Winton in script with MADE IN ENGLAND and letter A below.*

13. *1942+ Royal Winton in script with GRIMWADES MADE IN ENGLAND and letter A below.*

14. *1942+ Royal Winton in script with MADE IN ENGLAND and letter A below.*

15. *1942+ Royal Winton in script with GRIMWADES MADE IN ENGLAND.*

16. *1942+ Royal Winton in script with MADE IN ENGLAND.*

17. *1951+ Royal Winton in script with GRIMWADES MADE IN ENGLAND below set within lines.*

18. *1950s+ Crown above a large W with ROYAL WINTON below.*

19. *1964+ Royal Winton in fine script with GRIMWADES ENGLAND below.*

20. *1979+ J-W. Co with STAFFORDSHIRE ENGLAND. ROYAL WINTON curved below.*

21. *Atlas China 1910 onwards. Kneeling man supporting a globe (Atlas) with GRIMWADES across the globe. ATLAS CHINA STOKE ON TRENT above and ENGLAND below.*

22. *Rubian Art 1930+ RUBIAN above ART above POTTERY with ENGLAND curved below.*

23. *1930s+ Olde England. Rubian Art.*

24. *1929+ Anne Hathaway's Cottage.*

25. *1930s+ Shakespeare's Birthplace.*

26. *1934+ Ye Olde Inne.*

27. *1935+ Ye Olde Mill.*

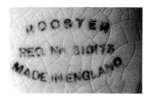

28. *1936+ Beehive.*

29. *1936+ Chanticleer.*

30. *1936+ Rooster.*

31. *1938+ Countryside.*

32. *1930s+ Crocus.*

33. *1934+ Gera.*

35. *1936+ Lakeland.*

34. *1936+ Lakeland.*

36. *1936+ Pixie.*

37 *1933+ Primula (Rubian Art).*

38. *1933+ Primula Hand Painted.*

39. *1933+ Regina.*

40. *1940s+ Briar.*

41. *1950s+ Honey Lily.*

42. *1940s+ Petunia.*

43. *1936+ Delphinium, signed W.H.*

44 *1930s+ Red Roof Hand Painted MADE IN ENGLAND.*

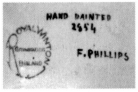

45. *1930s+ '6742' signed F. Phillips.*

46. *1930s+ '6742'.*

47. *1930s+ DEHLI with Handpainted below. Used in conjunction with Backstamp 4.*

48 *1930s+ RUBIAN WARE set in an artist's palette with HAND PAINTED above and DESIGNED BY IKE MATTISON below, all contained within a square.*

49. *1930s+ Handcraft in script above Backstamp 4.*

50. *1930s+ Hand Craft Pottery GRIMWADES LTD ENGLAND, all hand printed.*

51. *1925+ Byzanta Ware above Backstamp 1.*

52. *1930s. Carnation above Hand Painted, both in script with MADE IN ENGLAND below.*

53. *1925+ MING above diamond containing a dragon. GRIMWADES STOKE ON TRENT ENGLAND below.*

54 *1925+ Two figures in silhouette with BYZANTA WARE WATTEAU above and GRIMWADES ENGLAND below*

55. *1951+ COMOYS of London above Backstamp 12 but lacking the letter A.*

56. *Late 1930s+ Circular ROYAL WINTON mark with GENERAL DOUGLAS MACARTHUR above.*

57. *1931+ DICKENS above curved GRIMWADES ENGLAND.*

58 *1930s+ Oblong paper label typed Phil The Fluters Ball with THORENS Movement above and Made in Switzerland below. Also oval paper label with PRESENTA in gilt and black and GENUINE above and MUSICAL NOVELTY below.*

59. *1930s+ Masquerade Atlas China Stoke-on-Trent, all hand written.*

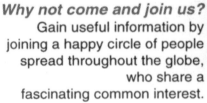

Francis Joseph
Collector's Register

Join the **Francis Joseph Royal Winton Collectors Register**. Registration is free and you will receive a newsletter twice yearly with news of special new limited edition pieces, auctions, events, sales and new publications on your particular collecting interest.

Join our register listing the type of items you collect, or call us and be placed on the register immediately.

The Francis Joseph Royal Winton
Collectors Register
5 Southbrook Mews, London SE12 8LG
Tel: 0181 318 9580